METROPOLITAN GOVERNANCE IN AMERICA

For Cheryl
With all my love

In Memory of
Don Phares

Metropolitan Governance in America

DONALD F. NORRIS
University of Maryland, Baltimore County, USA

ASHGATE

© Donald F. Norris 2015

All rights reserved. No part of this publication may be reproduced, stored in a retrieval system or transmitted in any form or by any means, electronic, mechanical, photocopying, recording or otherwise without the prior permission of the publisher.

Donald F. Norris has asserted his right under the Copyright, Designs and Patents Act, 1988, to be identified as the author of this work.

Published by
Ashgate Publishing Limited
Wey Court East
Union Road
Farnham
Surrey, GU9 7PT
England

Ashgate Publishing Company
110 Cherry Street
Suite 3-1
Burlington, VT 05401-3818
USA

www.ashgate.com

British Library Cataloguing in Publication Data
A catalogue record for this book is available from the British Library

The Library of Congress has cataloged the printed edition as follows:

Norris, Donald F.
  Metropolitan governance in America / by Donald F. Norris.
     pages cm
  Includes bibliographical references and index.
  ISBN 978-1-4094-2192-4 (hardback) -- ISBN 978-1-4094-2193-1 (ebook) -- ISBN 978-1-4724-0545-6 (epub) 1. Metropolitan government--United States. I. Title.
  JS422.N67 2015
  320.8'50973--dc23

2015006540

ISBN: 978-1-4094-2192-4 (HBK)
        978-1-4094-2193-1 (EBK)
        978-1-4724-0545-6 (EPUB)

 Printed in the United Kingdom by Henry Ling Limited, at the Dorset Press, Dorchester, DT1 1HD

Contents

List of Tables		*vii*
Preface		*ix*
1	Introduction	1
2	The Metropolitan Reform School	7
3	Public Choice Theory	35
4	The New Regionalism	59
5	Metropolitan Governance Survey	79
6	A Look at the Evidence	99
7	Conclusion	121
Index		*141*

List of Tables

Table 5.1	Response rate and representativeness	80
Table 5.2	Does metropolitan governance occur in your metro area?	85
Table 5.3	Do formal units of cooperation exist in your metro area?	86
Table 5.4	Is cooperation mostly formal or informal?	86
Table 5.5	How widespread is cooperation?	87
Table 5.6	Cooperation over systems maintenance or lifestyle functions	88
Table 5.7	Organizations in cooperative ventures	88
Table 5.8	Effectiveness of metro cooperation	89
Table 5.9	Size and metro cooperation	91
Table 5.10	Size and formal units of cooperation	91
Table 5.11	Size and formal or informal cooperation	92
Table 5.12	Size and how widespread is cooperation	92
Table 5.13	Functions of cooperation	93
Table 5.14	Organizations in cooperative ventures	94
Table 5.15	Effectiveness of cooperation	94
Table 6.1	Regional approaches to service delivery	100
Table 6.2	City–County consolidations in the US—1947–2010	113

Preface

This book is the culmination of a very long journey that began in the late 1960s at the University of Virginia. It was then that I took a course on urban politics as part of my graduate studies in political science in the Woodrow Wilson Department of Government and Politics at UVA.[1] There, for the first time, I was exposed to the writings of the Metro Reformers and their calls for serious governmental reform in America's metropolitan areas to deal with suburban sprawl, governmental fragmentation and the negative externalities of both that were affecting those areas and their residents throughout the nation. Naively, and more or less uncritically, I accepted the Metro Reformers' writings at face value and wondered why in the world the governments and residents of our metropolitan areas were refusing to heed the Metro Reformers' warnings and recommendations.

Had I only paid more attention when I was growing up in a rural town a few miles east of Rochester, New York, in the 1940s and 1950s, I might have known the answer. It turns out that my parents and our neighbors were part of the problem. In 1946, Charles Norris (a Second World War Veteran) and his wife Nina (and I), moved into a rented apartment in a house owned by a local farmer on Drum Road in the Town of Webster[2] for a short stay while waiting for their house on Klem Road, a mile or so away, to be built. The house, into which they (and I) moved in 1947, was on 30 acres of what had been a farm that was bounded by Klem Road to the south, the tracks of a spur line of the New York Central Railroad to the north, Van Alstyne Road to the east, and the Hembrook farm (around 50 acres) to the west. Except for their small, one-story, two-bedroom, one-bath house and a small barn behind it, there were no other structures on their land.

In the late 1940s, the Town of Webster was almost exclusively rural, with numerous fruit orchards, farms and dairies, the small, incorporated Village of Webster and the even smaller unincorporated hamlet of West Webster. In 1940, the Town population (including the Village) was 5,250 souls. By 1950, although the population had risen by more than one-third (36.6 percent) to 7,174, Webster remained mostly rural. Within a short time, however, Webster's rural character began giving way to that of a burgeoning bedroom suburb of Rochester.

My parents helped facilitate this transition by subdividing a sizeable portion of their 30 acres and selling individual building lots of an acre or two, which were nearly all snapped up by the mid-1950s, mainly by families moving out of Rochester. These newcomers to Webster wanted green spaces, good schools and

---

1   Now the Woodrow Wilson Department of Politics.

2   Counties in New York State are divided into Towns (aka, Townships in other states). Monroe County, NY, in which Webster is located, has 20 towns, the city of Rochester and several incorporated villages.

safe neighborhoods for their kids and themselves and, of course, lower taxes. They also wanted nothing more to do with the problems of the city that they had just left. Between 1950 and 1960, Webster's population more than doubled (129 percent growth), ballooning to 16,434, and the Town was having difficulty keeping up with the demand for public services, especially schools.

In subsequent decades, the Town's population continued to grow with farm after farm and orchard after orchard growing houses instead of fruit and vegetables. By 2010, the Town population was 42,641, a six-fold increase (494 percent) over 1950.[3] Webster's transformation, of course, was replicated throughout urban America during the decades following the Second World War.

A few years after completing graduate studies and still enamored of the Metro Reformers, I served as a consultant to a local television station in Grand Rapids, Michigan, in the production of a six-part documentary "At Issue: Metro Consolidation."[4] Needless to say, the documentary repeated many of the Metro Reformers' warnings and recommendations. Later, I led an effort through a business organization in Grand Rapids to secure an amendment to the Michigan state constitution that would permit county home rule. After three years of getting nowhere and in the face of opposition from just about every political source in the state, we gave up. Nevertheless, and even with this dose of political reality, I continued to wonder why, if things were as bad as the reformers said, local governments and their residents did not embrace reform. Clearly, the lessons that I should have learned in Webster continued to elude me.

Owing to changes in my career trajectory, I moved away from urban studies for a number of years, returning to the field in the late 1980s. As I began reacquainting myself with the issue of metropolitan governance, I came across the early works of the New Regionalists. Their argument, upon which I will elaborate in greater detail in Chapter 4, is that local governments in metro areas are impelled by forces beyond their control to cooperate with one another in order for their regions to be economically competitive in the global economy. I was then, and to this day remain, skeptical of this line of argument, but still I wondered if there was any truth to this argument, why did local governments not seem to be any more cooperative with one another than they were prior to the arrival of the New Regionalists?

As I continued reading and re-reading works on metropolitan governance, I began to think about research questions on this subject and also about ways in which I could contribute to this field of scholarship. As a result, since the early 1990s, I have conducted considerable research into and have written a number of journal articles, book chapters and conference papers about metropolitan governance, both in general and also tied to specific locations—the Baltimore, Maryland region, two conurbations in England and a comparison of metro governance in the US and Poland.

---

3   Even today, Webster is Rochester's fastest growing suburb. See: http://www.mapquest.com/us/ny/webster. Accessed December 20, 2014.

4   I moved to Grand Rapids in 1970 where I took my first academic position after completing graduate school.

Ultimately, my journey led to the writing of this book, although the book was also the beneficiary of a bit of serendipity. My colleague, friend and co-conspirator on several works on this subject, Don Phares, and I proposed a paper on metro governance for the 2009 European Urban Research Association (EURA) conference in Madrid. The paper was accepted, but, due to the Great Recession and university budget cuts, we were unable to attend the conference. Here is where serendipity comes in. Owing to the timing of budget cuts at our universities, we withdrew rather late from the conference—too late for our names and the title of our proposed paper to be removed from the program. Valerie Rose of Ashgate Publishing saw our entry in the program and emailed asking if we might be interested in writing a book on this subject for Ashgate to publish. Don and I submitted a proposal for the book, and, in the summer of 2010 we signed a contract to write it. After a number of twists and turns, and, sadly, after Don Phares had to withdraw from co-authoring because of health issues, I am pleased to say that it is finished.[5]

A long journey indeed. Moreover, as readers will note, the callow, naive and uncritical believer in Metro Reform has (he believes!) matured and has become a more skeptical consumer of writings that advocate metropolitan reform and governance. Read on and you will see.

Before moving on to the substance of the book, however, I want to thank several persons who assisted along the way. First and foremost, I want to thank Don Phares for our long collaboration on the subject of metropolitan governance. Together, Don and I engaged in close to a gazillion discussions about metro governance, sat on nearly as many panels at conferences, and wrote two book chapters and three conference papers on metro governance, all of which, in one way or another, fed into the writing of the book.[6]

Second, over the gestation period of the book and other works that I wrote on metropolitan government that preceded it, I have been assisted by five graduate research assistants from UMBC School of Public Policy, without whose efforts this project undoubtedly would have taken much longer and would not be nearly as good. So, thank you Aynur Saygun, Gretchen Shaub, Nicole Stewart and Tonya Zimmerman, especially for your labors in the vineyard of literature review. I am very grateful for all of your fine work. I also want to thank Lukas Glos for painstakingly reviewing the final manuscript to make sure that all citations and references were correct and that all direct quotations were accurate. Finally, let me thank Val Rose for suggesting this book and for so graciously weathering delays along the path of its writing. What we thought at the time would be a two-year effort has taken four and a half. But, here it is!

Donald F. Norris
Columbia, Maryland

---

5   More sadly, still, my dear friend Don Phares passed away in June of 2015, just months before the publication of this book. Because of our many discussions on the topic of metropolitan governance, I know that Don would agree with the contents and conclusions of this book. His memory lives on in its pages.

6   I also co-authored chapters that appeared in two books on metro governance that Don edited.

Chapter 1
Introduction

The United States is, for better or worse, awash in governments, local governments especially—89,004 of them in 2012 to be more or less precise (Census Bureau, 2012). Of these, 3,031 are counties, 19,522 are municipalities (cities, towns, villages and the like), 16,364 are townships (mainly in New England and the Midwest), 37,203 are special purpose governments (aka, special districts), and 12,884 are independent school districts. The nation also has 381 metropolitan areas (aka, metropolitan *statistical* areas, metro areas or MSAs).[1]

The federal Office of Management and Budget (OMB) defines a metropolitan area as a geographic territory that has an urban core with a population of at least 50,000, plus a surrounding territory that is socially and economically integrated with the central core. MSAs are statistical artifacts and have no standing in law, but are nevertheless important for an understanding of a wide variety of problems and issues in the nation's urbanized areas.

For the most part, the governance of US metro areas is highly fragmented, with numerous local governments of various types co-existing within them. Local governments' boundaries often overlap one another, especially special purpose governments whose boundaries overlap those of general-purpose governments. Local governments in metro areas often duplicate one another, in that many of them provide the same or very similar services but in smaller sub-areas of the larger metropolitan area. And, as I noted above, there are many, many local governments in the typical metro area.

Why is metropolitan governance important, and why should it be the subject of yet another book? It is important, first, because a significant proportion of our population, about 84 percent, lives in metro areas. Second, this population concentration means that it is in metro areas where we observe the largest number of and often the most intractable *urban* problems and issues, which, for decades, scholars and activists have examined and railed more or less unsuccessfully against. These are problems that flow primarily from the negative externalities of uncontrolled growth and development in metro areas and the suburban sprawl and governmental fragmentation that such growth and development beget. In the chapters that follow, I will touch on these problems, at least insofar as they have been identified in more than 85 years of study of the problems of American metropolitan areas.

---

1 Throughout the book I use the terms metropolitan area, metro area and region synonymously.

My main purpose in this book, however, is not to dissect the problems of metro areas, but, instead, it is to address the question of whether metropolitan governance exists in the US. If so, under what circumstances it does it exist, and, if not, why, and then whether is it even possible to argue that metropolitan governance is likely to develop. This, in turn, is important because, since at least 1930, scholars, advocates and other observers have been calling for significant governmental reform in metropolitan areas and for the development of metropolitan governance to address the negative externalities caused by uncontrolled growth, sprawl and fragmentation.

In this chapter, I begin my examination of metropolitan governance with a definition of the term itself. I do so, in part, because few, if any, other works on this subject explicitly define metropolitan governance. Instead, many such works either assume that everyone "knows it when they see it" or allow a very broad understanding of the term—so broad that virtually anything (for example, the most limited acts of intergovernmental cooperation) is often viewed as governance.

To me, governance means something more than cooperation, and metropolitan governance means governance across an entire region. I define this term as:

> The formal association of governments, non-governmental organizations and/ or residents in a metropolitan area for the purpose of controlling or regulating behavior and/or performing functions or services within the metropolitan area. Governance is areawide, governing decisions are binding, and participants can be compelled to comply with them. (This expands on the definition in Norris, 2001.)

This definition is consistent with both standard dictionary definitions and the traditional understanding of governance that comes from the discipline of political science—governance as regulation and control.

Webster's Dictionary (1987: p. 529) defines *governance* as *government*, and it defines the latter as "the act or process of governing; specifically, authoritative direction and control." It defines the verb *to govern* as "to exercise continuous sovereign authority," and "to control and direct the making and administration of policy," among other things. To govern also means "holding in check" and "restraining" (presumably behavior).

Noted political scientist David Easton (1965) argued that one of the principal functions of a political system is " ... the authoritative allocation of values for society." Easton's concept of authoritative allocation means two fundamentally important things. First, decisions flow from proper authority and, therefore, are legitimate (*authoritative*). Second, they are binding on all participants (the entire society) and must be obeyed. Anything less and decisions are meaningless because they do not affect all members of a society and have no teeth and cannot be enforced.

I contrast metropolitan governance with metropolitan cooperation and define the latter term as:

> The voluntary association of governments, non-governmental organizations and/or residents within a metropolitan area for purposes of addressing issues of mutual concern and/or performing functions and services. Cooperation may be areawide or may involve territory less than areawide. Cooperation may involve as few as two organizations or as many as all of the organizations in the area. Cooperation may involve one issue, function or service or many. Because cooperation is voluntary, decisions taken are not authoritative, and participants cannot be compelled to comply with them. (This expands on the definition in Norris 2001).

According to *Webster's*, cooperation means: "1) to act or work with one another or others; work together: 2) associate with one another or others for mutual benefit" (288). Thus, cooperation is not governance. As I will explain later, cooperation is no doubt better than conflict, but it cannot substitute for governance for it lacks the ability to compel compliance with decisions mutually taken.

The reality of metropolitan politics is that, while governments in these areas do, in fact, cooperate with one another around a number of services, functions and issues, they are loath to surrender any of their presumed autonomy in order to address the really tough, controversial issues that flow from the negative externalities of growth, sprawl and fragmentation. Thus, these areawide issues are rarely confronted in meaningful ways. The unwillingness of local governments to coalesce and address these problems produces very uneven patterns of metropolitan development, with some territories flourishing and others languishing. With some exceptions, newer and more distant suburbs are doing well while central cities and older, near-in suburbs are doing relatively poorly by nearly every measure.

I urge the reader to bear my definitions of governance and cooperation in mind as she or he reads on. To assist that reading, let me briefly outline the structure of the book that follows.

In Chapter 2, I focus on the works of the Metro Reformers—specifically 18 works by scholars, advocates and advocacy organizations, and the long since defunct US Advisory Commission on Intergovernmental Relations. These works are notable for at least four reasons. First, the identification of problems associated with the fragmented nature of government and the uncontrolled growth occurring in metropolitan areas. Second, the identification of negative externalities flowing from these problems. Third, the (mainly, although not exclusively) structural reforms recommended to address the negative externalities. Fourth, the extraordinary degree of consistency among the authors of these works about the problems of fragmentation and sprawl, the negative externalities that they produce and the range of solutions available to address them. It is also noteworthy that most of these works lacked the empirical evidence that modern scholars might require before making such wide ranging and substantial recommendations for governmental change.

Chapter 3 is my critical assessment of yet another school of thought around the subject of metro governance. This school, however, holds a position that is diametrically the opposite of the Metro Reformers and the New Regionalists. The Public Choice School argues that the sprawling, fragmented metro area is fine just as it is because it acts as a quasi-market mechanism in which the local governments in a metropolitan area, acting in a manner similar to that of firms competing in the marketplace. Here, local governments offer distinct packages of goods or services to prospective consumers (or citizens). This, in turn, provides those customers with the unfettered opportunity to make choices among many different residential locations and to select the one that best meets their personal preferences. As such, there is no need for regional anything—governance or cooperation.

In this chapter, I examine what is undoubtedly the single most influential work in the history of this school—Charles Tiebout's (1956) theoretical model of the behavior of local governments and citizens in metropolitan areas. I do so to understand the model's assumptions because they provide the very foundation of the school. If the model's assumptions are not empirically correct (that is, if they do not present an accurate view of how local governments and residents of metropolitan areas actually behave), the model itself will fail. In my analysis of the model, I also employ the works of a number of scholars who have preceded me in critically examining this model.

In Chapter 4, I address the New Regionalism, and I do so in much the same way I addressed the Metro Reformers in Chapter 2. That is, through the principal works of scholars in this school. Here, however, I am particularly interested in the assumptions and arguments underlying these works insofar as they either provided a solid foundation for the claims made by New Regionalist writers or they did not. For example, can voluntary cooperation be an effective substitute for governmental structures? Do local governments in American regions, in fact, compete in the global economy? For reasons of economic survival, are they, therefore, impelled to cooperate with one another to address the negative externalities identified in both the Metro Reform and New Regionalist literature? Or, does politics trump economics, preventing these governments from cooperating except on the margins? And, last, are suburbs dependent on their (often declining) central cities for their own (the suburbs') economic success, and, if so, will suburban governments be more likely to cooperate with their central cities for the sake of the economic survival of the overall region in the global economy? I also examine case studies of metro governance both in the US and abroad to broaden my study of the New Regionalism and to ask if metro governance as proposed by the New Regionalists exists anywhere.

Next, in Chapter 5, I report the findings of a survey that I conducted among the Councils of Government in the nation's largest 102 metropolitan areas. In this survey, I asked a number of questions about metropolitan governance and cooperation. It will come as little surprise to readers that I found a considerable array of cooperation but precious little governance among these regions. Yes, local governments in metro areas cooperate, but they generally do not cooperate over the tough, controversial issues that confront their areas. Nor do they engage in metro-wide governance over virtually anything, although I did find evidence of sub-regional governance around certain issues (notably, but not exclusively, transportation).

In Chapter 6, I examine the evidence, beyond the survey, that local governments in metro areas have actually adopted any of the reforms suggested by the Metro Reformers and the New Regionalists that are likely to have a substantial impact on addressing the negative externalities of fragmentation and sprawl. Here, I find that the local governments have, indeed, adopted a number of recommended reforms, but almost exclusively the easy ones. And the easy ones are hardly likely to enable regions to ameliorate the negative externalities of growth, fragmentation and sprawl.

In the concluding chapter, Chapter 7, I ask why there is virtually no metropolitan governance in the US and very little meaningful intergovernmental cooperation to address these externalities. The answer lies in politics. For a number of reasons that I think are not only readily understandable but patently obvious, local governments will not work together in ways that will enable them to address the negative externalities of fragmentation and sprawl. While local governments in metro areas cooperate over a wide variety of issues, they rarely do so in ways that enable them to address truly metro-wide problems and issues. This is because local governments are not willing to surrender any part of their budgets or autonomy in order to serve the needs of the overall territory.

Indeed, the failure of local governments in metro areas to address the tough areawide issues is historic and has been well documented for at least 85 years. Moreover, all or nearly all of the factors that prevent these governments from doing so are political. I discuss these political factors and show how they operate to keep local governments from addressing the negative externalities of fragmentation and sprawl.

I briefly examine a growing body of literature on *network governance*, that examines the contingencies of governmental cooperation. I also briefly review the literature on *incremental regionalism*. These literatures may offer some hope that local governments, if only on the margins, can come together to address common issues and problems. I am not, however, very sanguine here because of the overwhelming evidence I have presented in this book that local governments will not work together to address the really tough issues that confront nearly all metro areas in the US.

Finally, I argue that what we observe in America's metropolitan areas today on the subject of metropolitan governance and what has been observed and recorded over decades past, is almost certainly what we will also observe in decades to come. There is no metropolitan governance and, for the reasons discussed herein, metropolitan governance is most unlikely to begin to develop. Better we seek ways to secure intergovernmental cooperation, than to advocate or wish for metropolitan governance. The former may be the weakest means to address metro problems, but pursuing the latter is a fool's errand.

References

Easton, David. 1965. *A Systems Analysis of Political Life*. New York: Wiley.

Norris, Donald F. 2001. Prospects for regional governance under the new regionalism: Economic imperatives versus political impediments. *Journal of Urban Affairs*, 23(5): 557–571. Special issue entitled, "Regionalism Reconsidered."

Tiebout, Charles. 1956. A pure theory of local expenditures. *Journal of Political Economy*, 64(5): 416–424.

US Bureau of the Census. 2012. *Census of Governments 2012*. https://www.census.gov/newsroom/releases/archives/governments/cb12–161.html. Accessed November 22, 2014.

Webster's Ninth New Collegiate. 1987. Springfield, MA: Merriam-Webster, Inc., Publishers.

Chapter 2
The Metropolitan Reform School

In this chapter, I examine works from what is called the Metropolitan Reform School of metropolitan government and governance. The great majority of works that emanated from this school were published between the late 1950s and mid-1970s in the form of books, journal articles, reports or other monographs. The works of this school are similar in five important ways. First, the authors of these works identified problems associated with the growth of metropolitan areas. Second, they identified the negative externalities that they claimed flowed from these problems. Third, they recommended both structural and non-structural alternatives to address the negative externalities (although they clearly favored the structural over the non-structural). Fourth, there is a high degree of consistency among these authors and their works regarding the problems of metropolitan growth, the negative externalities flowing from them and the solutions to address the negative externalities. Finally, for the most part, these works were arguments or advocacy pieces supported by little evidence, and their authors proceeded normatively rather than empirically, especially regarding the issue of the preferences of the residents of metropolitan areas.[1]

Additionally, there is a great deal of agreement between the writings of the Metro Reformers and the New Regionalists regarding the problems of metro areas and the externalities flowing from those problems. However, the two schools part in terms of their recommended solutions. I will address this further in Chapter 4.

In the pages that follow in this chapter, I examine many if not most of the major works of the Metro Reformers, and I do so chronologically. These works are:

- Paul Studenski. 1930. *The Government of Metropolitan Areas in the United States*
- Victor Jones. 1942, *Metropolitan Government*
- Luther Gulick. 1957. Metropolitan organization. (In the *Annals of the American Academy of Political and Social Sciences*)
- Robert C. Wood. 1957. Metropolitan government 1975: An extrapolation of trends. The new metropolis: Green belts, grass roots or Gargantua. (In the *American Political Science Review*)
- Robert C. Wood. 1958. *Suburbia: Its People and Its Politics*

---

1 However, I suspect that, if asked, many of these writers would say that they proceeded rationally—by which they meant that they eschewed emotion and silly things like preferences and examined problems as engineers might!

8   *Metropolitan Governance in America*

- Chamber of Commerce of the United States. 1960. *Modernizing Local Government*
- Robert C. Wood. 1961. *1400 Governments: The Political Economy of the New York Metropolitan Region*
- US Advisory Commission on Intergovernmental Relations. 1961. *Governmental Structure, Organization, and Planning in Metropolitan Areas*
- Scott A. Greer. 1962. *Governing the Metropolis*
- US Advisory Commission on Intergovernmental Relations. 1962. *Alternative Approaches to Governmental Reorganization in Metropolitan Areas*[2]
- Roscoe C. Martin. 1963. *Metropolis in Transition: Local Government Adaptation to Changing Urban Needs*. (A report for the US Housing and Home Finance Agency)
- Luther H. Gulick. 1966. *The Metropolitan Problem and American Ideas*
- US Advisory Commission on Intergovernmental Relations. 1966. *Metropolitan America; Challenge to Federalism*
- Chamber of Commerce of the United States. 1967 (replacing report of same title dated 1960). *Modernizing Local Government*
- US Advisory Commission on Intergovernmental Relations. 1969. *Urban America and the Federal System*
- Committee for Economic Development. 1970. *Reshaping Government in Metropolitan Areas*
- US Advisory Commission on Intergovernmental Relations. 1973–1974. *Substate Regionalism and the Federal System*. Volume I: Regional Decision Making: New Strategies for Substate Districts. October, 1973
- US Advisory Commission on Intergovernmental Relations. 1977. *Regionalism revisited: Recent areawide and local responses. A brief update of the Commission's series of reports on substate regionalism and the federal system published in 1973–73*

Readers will note that the first two works I review, however, considerably pre-dated the time frame in which most of the Metro Reform works were published. Paul Studenski's *The Government of Metropolitan Areas in the United States*, written as a report for the National Municipal League, was published in 1930,

---

2   ACIR also published a number of additional works that, in part, supported its various reports and recommendations on governmental restructuring in metropolitan areas. These included reports on determining which governmental functions should be performed at the local and areawide levels (1963), social and economic disparities in metropolitan areas (1965), metropolitan fiscal disparities (1967), the problem of special district governments (1964), factors affecting voter reaction to metro government reorganization proposals, For purposes of this chapter, I chose only those works that are directly relevant to governmental reform and restructuring in metro areas. Readers should also be aware that ACIR published numerous works on a wide range of intergovernmental subjects, many of which did not address governmental reform or restructuring in metro areas at all.

nearly three decades before the writings of the Metro Reformers began to appear. The second, Victor Jones's *Metropolitan Government* was published in 1942. Clearly, then, at least in the minds of some observers, the problems of metropolitan America predated the post-Second World War era, even though it was in that period that the problems of metropolitan America received the greatest amount of focused attention.

In this chapter, I follow a simple template and focus on four issues in each of the works I reviewed: 1) What did the writers say were the principal problems associated with population growth in American metropolitan areas? 2) What did they say were the principal negative externalities produced by these problems? 3) What solutions did they propose? 4) What did they say, if anything, about the ease or difficulty of their proposed solutions being adopted? Thus, my reviews are not full and complete reviews of each work, as one might expect of a book review. Instead, they are focused narrowly on only these four issues. I wish to make this clear because several of the works I reviewed are more wide-ranging and comprehensive than these four issues would suggest.

Paul Studenski. 1930. *The Government of Metropolitan Areas in the United States*

Studenski's work is notable for a number of reasons, not the least of which is because it was remarkably prescient. The problems that Studenski identified, the negative externalities flowing from them that he catalogued, the range of solutions that he recommended to address them and his take on the ease or difficulty of getting them adopted have been echoed repeatedly throughout the later Metro Reform literature and also in the New Regionalist literature.

Studenski began by noting several common problems that metro areas (by which he meant both the governments and the citizens of those areas) faced in 1930. His list was extensive and included:

- traffic, transportation;
- water supply;
- wastewater management;
- solid waste;
- light and power service;
- public health and hospitals;
- planning;
- law enforcement;
- fire service;
- parks and recreation;
- education;
- local government finance; and
- fiscal and wealth disparities.

He argued that these problems were areawide or metropolitan in nature and, as such, " ... can only be solved through a plan embracing the whole area or large sections of it" (31).

After noting these problems, he addressed the organization of metropolitan areas in terms of their capacity to address the problems. He wrote that although these areas were extraordinarily complex,

> The political organization of metropolitan areas can best be described as no organization at all, but a mere conglomeration of political divisions of various kinds, established at various times, and not bounded together in any way (23).

Moreover, Studenski noted that as metro areas grew, so, too, did the number of local governments within them, creating yet another negative externality: governmental fragmentation. Furthermore, because of the fragmented governmental structure of metro areas, little or no capacity existed to address what were, in his view, areawide problems.

As for why little or no capacity existed to address areawide problems, he placed the blame squarely on the local governments within these areas.

> The political subdivisions are jealous of each other and proceed in virtual independence. Each has its own executive and legislative organizations, its traditions, policies, political issues. Frequently each political unit enjoys some special advantage which it desires to retain and which causes it to assume an attitude of suspicion towards other sections not possessed of such advantage; or it labors under some special disadvantage which causes it to envy other communities not under like handicap. It is difficult under these conditions to bring about concerted action throughout the metropolitan area. Consequently it is often well-nigh impossible to solve effectively municipal problems common to all (29).

For Studenski, the solutions to the inability of metro areas to address areawide problems were almost exclusively structural and were based on the concept of "integration," something to which later Metro Reformers returned frequently.

> For this task [addressing areawide problems] it is necessary that localities be integrated in such a manner as will enable the whole region to function as a political unit. The integration must be so effected as to foster the development of a vigorous metropolitan consciousness throughout, preserve and cultivate a healthy consciousness of locality in the constituent parts, and secure the proper treatment of purely local as distinguished from metropolitan affairs (41).

The principal mechanisms that he recommended for producing integration included:[3]

- voluntary or forced cooperation;
- annexation (voluntary and forcible);
- consolidation of neighboring municipalities;
- city–county consolidation;
- expansion of the services of county government (the precursor to the urban county);
- extension of municipal services beyond the boundaries of the central city;
- special districts; and
- federated government (the precursor to the two-tier government).[4]

Studenski followed this listing with supporting arguments for the need for integration and further discussion of the need for areawide mechanisms to address the negative externalities of metropolitan growth. In the remaining chapters of the book, he addressed each of his proposed solutions.

At the end of the day, however, Studenski was not sanguine about the likelihood that these solutions would be adopted. He noted early in the book that, "… instances of joint enterprise between cities are relatively few" (51). This, he argued, was mainly because local governments themselves do not want to take such action unless their own self-interests are satisfied. Finally, in the concluding chapter, he lamented that these solutions had little chance of being adopted without considerable change in the way that local politicians and civic leaders [I would add citizens—although this was almost certainly implicit in Studenski's writing] envision the metro area and act upon that envisioning. They must, he said, stop thinking in terms of their local governments first and then (or hardly ever) the overall region.

In nearly every way imaginable, Studenski created the intellectual path for subsequent Metro Reformers to follow and expand upon, which they did with great fervor.

Victor Jones. 1942. *Metropolitan Government*

Like Studenski, Jones argued that while individual local governments are appropriate for the governance of small jurisdictions, when combined they constituted "… a single metropolitan community" (xix). He further noted,

---

3 For readers who are unfamiliar with the various alternatives proposed by the Metro Reformers, please refer to Table 6.1 in Chapter 6.

4 A federated, or two-tier government is one in which the lower level handles what are deemed local functions and services while the upper level handles what are deemed to be areawide functions and services. Studenski noted that the federated approach had been considered by Boston, MA (1896), Alameda, CA (1922) and Pittsburgh, PA (1926), but had not been adopted in any of these three regions.

however, that there was no "... metropolitan coverage of essential functions and services" (xx). As such, there was a need for the "... realignment of boundaries between, and the reallocation of functions among, all levels of government" (xx). As readers will note in due course, the need for realignment (by this and other terms) became a standard claim in the later metro reform literature.[5]

Among the problems that led to the need for metro reform, which Jones first identified, were the large number of individual local governments (cities, counties, suburban municipalities, special districts) in metro areas (aka, governmental fragmentation) and the jealousies among local governments, none of which alone is able to address areawide problems.

> The problem of metropolitan government may be described as the need for servicing a large population scattered under the jurisdiction of many units of local government, most of which are crippled by limited powers over a restricted areas, by inadequate tax resources, and by such consequences of premature subdivision as heavy indebtedness and extensive tax arrears (24).

Jones identified several discrete service problems that he argued were areawide in nature, including:

- drainage;
- water supply and distribution;
- metro transit;
- sewage and solid waste;
- water pollution;
- public health;
- police;
- fire fighting;
- disparities in wealth (and, as a result, of tax revenue);
- disparities in serviced delivery; and
- disparities of need.

He also noted the lack of cooperation among local governments due to jealousy and suspicion.

Jones suggested both non-structural and structural reforms as potential solutions to these problems. Non-structural solutions included:

- extraterritorial power and service provision;
- special districts;[6]
- intergovernmental cooperation;

---

5 Realignment means making decisions about which functions properly belong to the local or the metropolitan level of government (for example, county, metro, and so on).

6 Although Jones listed special districts in the non-structural category, most of the later Metro Reformers and most scholars today would consider them structural.

- state takeover or assumption of metro functions (for example, sanitation, water supply, transportation, health, police, and others, with examples from various metro areas); and
- greater federal involvement (also with a variety of examples).

Structural solutions included:

- annexation;
- consolidation;
- mergers of special districts with city or county governments;
- the urban county;
- federation; and
- creation of city-states for the largest metros (for example, NY, Chicago, Detroit, where proposals for such had previously been put forward although not adopted).

Concerning support or opposition to integration by central cities, Jones noted that business interests, labor organizations, and politicians "… can find equal reason to be on either side of the question" (294). At the same time, however, "City officials are much less opposed to city-county separation than to metropolitan schemes of local government integration" (294).

Regarding the likelihood of suburbs supporting any proposals for metro reform, he wrote:

> Most of the suburban opposition to integration with the central city seems to be expressed by suburban politicians and suburban publishers … But it would be a mistake to assume that, on the whole, their constituents do not share their attitude (319).

In his concluding chapter, Jones noted the immense difficulty of achieving any of these proposed solutions because of the need to secure either "… legislative or electoral approval" (337).

On the whole, Jones's work closely followed Studenski's (which he cited extensively), and many of his observations and recommendations paralleled Studenski's. Taken together, both works set the standard for the later Metro Reformer literature.

Luther Gulick. 1957. Metropolitan Organization

Writing in the *Annals of the American Academy of Political and Social Sciences*, Luther Gulick cited what, by then, had become many of the "usual suspects"[7]

---

7 Clearly, there is some variation in the lists of "usual suspects" among different Metro Reformers, but there is greater similarity among most of them than there are differences.

of areawide problems caused by metropolitan growth (he and other writers also called these unmet needs) and that included:

- water supply;
- waste disposal;
- pollution control;
- education;
- housing;
- health;
- crime;
- flood protection;
- fire protection; and
- chaotic transportation system.

After identifying these problems, Gulick noted that individual local governments were unable to address them effectively, if at all. He then suggested four alternatives. The first was for states to create departments of local affairs with a metropolitan unit to focus on the problems of metro areas. Second, he called for the development of the urban or metropolitan county, which would have the powers needed to address areawide problems. Third, he proposed metropolitan service agencies that would perform from one to several areawide functions. (The metro service agency closely resembles a special district, which numerous reformers both called for and disliked—more on this in due course.) Finally, like Studenski and Jones before him, Gulick called for development of essentially a two-tier solution. He called his the Metropolitan Council, which would be a new layer of government and would handle all metro wide functions leaving the purely local functions to local governments.

As readers will note, there were very few differences, certainly none of consequence, between Studenski and Jones and later Gulick in terms of problem identification. However, Gulick's list of proposed reforms was somewhat less extensive than those of either Studenski or Jones.

Robert C. Wood. 1957. Metropolitan Government 1975: An Extrapolation

In this article, published in the *American Political Science Review*, Robert Wood discussed what he believed to be the three principal negative effects of sprawl. The first was the excessive cost of governing metropolitan areas because of duplication of services and overlapping jurisdictions and facilities as well as the loss of use of economies of scale. Second, he noted what he called "a deterioration of the political process," (110), by which he meant that the affluent depart central cities, which leaves those cities with a politics that pits the very rich against the very poor. Finally, he noted the bifurcation between central cities and their suburbs.

The Metropolitan Reform School

To address what he called the metro dilemma, Wood proposed a two-tier government.[8] Having proposed this reform, however, Wood also noted that:

> ... despite our predictions [of negative externalities], disaster has not struck: urban government has continued to function, not well perhaps, but at least well enough to forestall catastrophe. Traffic continues to circulate; streets and sewers are built; water is provided; schools keep their doors open; and law and order generally prevail. *Nor does this tolerable state of affairs result from an eager citizenry's acceptance of our counsel: we know only too well that our proposals for genuine reform have been largely ignored* (112). Emphasis added.

Nevertheless, like many a metro reformer, Wood argued that while metro areas may not face catastrophe, this should not be a reason to fail to address the negative consequences of metropolitan growth.

Robert C. Wood. 1958. *Suburbia: Its People and Its Politics*

Wood began by examining the rise of suburbs in the US in the years prior to the Second World War and continued to examine the nature and character of the suburbs in the post-Second World War period. Among other things, Wood observed that that expansion of the suburbs in this latter period resulted in the replication of small, autonomous local governments throughout metro areas in the United States. These governments, at least according to their detractors, were insufficient to the task of governance, especially of areawide problems such as those often listed by the metro reformers.

Wood acknowledged that, well before post-war suburbanization, reformers had advocated for annexation, transferring functions upward to counties, establishing multi-purpose special districts, and, finally, two-tier metropolitan governments. He, too, suggested that structural changes could be helpful, but admitted that they were unlikely to be implemented. He noted that, after considering reforms, "... as a rule, the suburbs were unimpressed ..." and most reform proposals came to naught (81).

> Annexation, consolidation, merger, country[sic]-city separation—suburbia considered all of them and usually concluded that it wanted none of them It preferred legal autonomy and small town politics above all, and it continued to expand (83).

---

8 So far in this chapter, I have noted that two-tier government was proposed by each of the authors reviewed. However, none of them identified any criteria or a process by which functions and services could be determined to be either areawide or local. This was true of nearly all of the Metro Reformers, except for the ACIR, especially its 1973–1974 report on substate regionalism, which I review later in this chapter.

16 *Metropolitan Governance in America*

One reason for this, Wood argued, was the absence of an "institutional base" from which to launch reform efforts and the opposition of suburban officials to reform. Moreover, there were few powerful actors anywhere who supported metro reform.

> So, the banner for reform is for the most part carried on by a thin rank of largely ineffective agitators—editorial writers in the metropolitan dailies, planners, professors, a few executives ..., the "public spirited," presidents of voluntary civic associations, a scattering of businessmen ..., perhaps the mayor, possibly the governor. This is an ill-assorted collection of interests and personalities unlikely to be strongly motivated, rarely possessing sufficient influence to carry the public with their ways and always ready to snatch at any plan that might take a half step forward (300).

Wood also noted that despite the problems faced by the small governments of suburbia:

> The longer the public problems of suburbia are studied, the more impressive become the qualities of suburban tenacity and inventiveness which preserve the grassroots in the face of the continuing challenges of modern life (254).

Even recognizing the reality that suburban governments persevere and that reform is exceptionally difficult to achieve (he called the latter "a genuine unpleasant fact"), Wood lamented: "It is too bad that there is little inclination to consider rationally the benefits that a gargantuan metropolitan government and social order might offer" (301).

Chamber of Commerce of the United States. 1960. *Modernizing Local Government*

In this short pamphlet, the US Chamber of Commerce, probably the leading representative and advocacy group of the nation's business community, addressed the capacity of local government to function effectively in the face of the tremendous population growth that was then occurring in metropolitan America. The Chamber's concerns were mainly related to service problems caused by that growth. Among other problems, the Chamber pointed to water, sewer, traffic congestion, streets and highways and hospitals. Addressing these problems, the Chamber argued, was difficult because, first, local governments were restricted by state law (or the lack thereof) in their ability to act on these problems, and, second, the multiple and often overlapping governmental jurisdictions in metro areas produced a form of rigidity where greater flexibility was needed.

The Chamber recognized that some alternatives were available to local governments including interlocal cooperation, contracting out and even metropolitan government, although these options were not being widely used. Interestingly, also, the Chamber also called for greater individual self-control. "If only people will exercise self-discipline in the demands they make upon their government, they can lessen the burdens of modernization" (12).

Robert C. Wood. 1961. *1400 Governments: The Political Economy of the New York Metropolitan Region*

Wood employed data from the New York metropolitan region to examine what he termed as this "vigorous" metropolitan area (1). One of his main concerns was how governmental fragmentation affected the ability of the region to function. As a result, his was not a book that advocated metro reform, as did so many works that preceded it. It was, rather, more of an analytical effort. As Wood put it:

> The state of fragmentation can be defended as carrying on the cherished democratic tradition of home rule. It can be deplored as hopelessly unsuited to the realities of modern life. Our purpose in this book is neither to defend nor to deplore but to observe, dissect and classify the Region's governments and to estimate their likely impact on the Region's development (1–2).

Nevertheless, some of its contents are worth attention for the purposes of this chapter. For example, Wood was well aware of the relationship between the movement of population from the center to the periphery and the sprawl that accompanied it. Indeed, he identified several problems that, he said, arose as a result of sprawl and fragmentation including:

- financial disparities;
- environmental damage;
- water;
- sanitation;
- transportation; and
- public welfare.

In addition, he noted that sprawl was also responsible for governmental fragmentation, which in the New York region had produced 1,467 local governments. Metropolitan growth patterns created a demand for public services in suburban areas, which in turn produced even more local governments. Wood illustrated the extreme fragmentation with the example of one county in New Jersey that included 70 different units of government.

Although the governments within the New York metropolitan area had similar needs, Wood argued that the extent of fragmentation made it nearly impossible for metro-wide problems to be addressed effectively. Fragmentation, he observed,

18   *Metropolitan Governance in America*

also resulted in need often being divorced from resources among the numerous local governments in the region.

Wood suggested only one structural reform in order to address the negative externalities of fragmentation, the regional enterprise. A regional enterprise was a single-purpose special district that would provide one service region-wide. Wood did not propose any other reforms.

Regarding the likelihood of governments in the region adopting reforms, he was pessimistic and felt that sweeping structural changes were not politically feasible.

> Thus, little opportunity exists for the development of Regionwide [sic] public policy. Each government is preoccupied with its own problems, and collectively the governments are not prepared to formulate general policies for guiding economic development, or to make generalized responses to the financial pressures generated by urbanization (113).

US Advisory Commission on Intergovernmental Relations. 1961.
Governmental Structure, Organization, and Planning in Metropolitan Areas

The purpose of this Advisory Commission on Intergovernmental Relations (ACIR) report was to make recommendations to state governments and the federal government regarding actions that they should take to address the intergovernmental problems arising in US metro areas. The report began by noting the population growth occurring in metro areas and also the complexity of local government structure in those areas, especially the multiple and overlapping governments. "Local governments in metropolitan areas present a bewildering pattern both because of their extreme numbers and their frequent territorial overlapping" (14). Among other things, this, then, resulted in problems in equity and efficient administration.

The report argued that state constitutional and statutory restrictions compounded the problems of local government structure by limiting the ability of local governments to respond and make necessary changes. The ACIR particularly noted that state constitutions and laws often limit the ability of cities to annex and, at the same time, make it reasonably easy to incorporate territories outside established municipalities. The report also noted that things were even more complicated in interstate metro areas, although in some areas interstate compacts had been successfully employed.

Next, the report made recommendations for state governments including:

- amend the notion of home rule to provide for both local and metro home rule with each available to address problems at either the local or metro level;
- enable municipal annexation of unincorporated territory without the consent of those being annexed;
- permit interlocal contracting and joint agreements;

The Metropolitan Reform School 19

- enable the creation of "functional authorities" (aka, multi-purpose special districts under greater accountability and citizen control;
- allow transfers of functions between and among cities and counties;
- allow the creation of metro area study commissions;
- permit the creation of metro area planning bodies;
- establish a unit within state government charged with addressing metropolitan affairs;
- states should provide direct financial and technical assistance to metro areas;
- states should to more to preserve open space in metro areas; and
- states should do more to resolve disputes in metro areas.

Then, the ACIR made recommendations to the federal government, including:

- provide financial assistance to metro planning agencies;
- provide technical assistance to metro planning agencies;
- Congress should adopt legislation proving advance approval of interstate compacts;
- Federal review of local government applications for certain federal grants (precursor to A-95 review);
- improve the coordination of federal grants and programs affecting metro areas; and
- create a federal Department of Urban Affairs.

The commission concluded, in part, by saying:

> The Commission believes that the problems of governmental structure, organization, planning, and cooperation are so urgent and critical as to require the ushering-in of an "era of reciprocal forbearance" among the units of government concerned (57).

In other words, local governments needed to cede power and autonomy to address the problems of the metropolitan area for the greater good of all.

Scott A. Greer. 1962. *Governing the Metropolis*

Strictly speaking, Greer was not a metro reformer. Indeed, the purpose of his book was not to advocate but to understand. He wrote, he said, "… to summarize many studies of politics and government in metropolitan areas" (vi). Therefore, and unlike many of the works of the metro reformers, he did not develop a list of the ailments of metro areas and prescribe solutions.

In the first few chapters of the book, Greer discussed how the metropolis came into being, described its principal characteristics and described the governance of metro areas including their central cities and suburbs. He particularly noted the schizoid nature of the metropolis, divided as it were between the central city and the suburbs and the problems that this division produced. "The governmental dichotomy of the metropolis and the fragmentation of the suburbs have serious consequences for the total urban complex" (107). He went on to say that the:

> ... fragmented polity confronts problems that are areawide in their origins, affecting all parts of the metropolitan area; they are problems which seem, logically and technically, to demand an areawide governmental response. Such a response, however, is difficult to imagine in an urban complex made up of a hundred or a thousand separate governmental jurisdictions (107–108).

He noted that reformers had proposed various solutions to the problem of fragmentation, and most of these were based on the principle of integration. Three of the reformers' favorite solutions were the urban county, a two-tier or federated system and irredentism ("... the return the lost territories of suburbia to their rightful polity, the central city" (120)). However, reform efforts mainly did not succeed. "The results have been failure, in city after city, time after time. This failure reflects the existing dichotomy of the metropolis and the resulting political schizophrenia" (122).

He noted the following barriers to metro reform:

> 1) The underlying cultural norms of Americans concerning local government—suburban residents value smaller local government in that it allows community members the power to design and maintain their neighborhoods, 2) the resulting legal-constitutional structures, which result from the desire to maintain smaller local governments, provide even weak local governments with the autonomy to control decisions made in their immediate municipality, and 3) the political-governmental system built upon them (124).

As a result, the very political system, of which metro areas and their constituents are a part, militates against reform.

Regardless of the problems that fragmentation produces, however, Greer argued that: "The metropolis is in little danger of breakdown" (129). This was because, constrained as they were, metro areas had "... room to maneuver" (130). By this, he meant that there were alternatives to integration that enabled local governments in metro areas to address the problems that they confronted. Among others, the alternatives included voluntary cooperation, joint planning, contractual arrangements and the use of special districts.

He concluded by noting that metropolitan areas were works in progress. They were in a state of continual improvisation and evolution, developing organically rather than rationally and that change would occur, not in a revolutionary way.

US Advisory Commission on Intergovernmental Relations. 1962. *Alternative Approaches to Governmental Reorganization in Metropolitan Areas*

This was a supplement to and an extension of the 1961 report entitled *Governmental Structure, Organization, and Planning in Metropolitan Areas*.

The report began by noting that uncontrolled growth in metropolitan areas had produced sprawl and congestion, and the fragmented structure of local government in metro areas meant that it was increasingly difficult to address areawide service needs, such as: mass transit and traffic, water supply and distribution, sewage and solid waste disposal, air pollution, open space preservation and civil defense. Fragmentation had also resulted in disparities in taxes and services—mainly a disparity between aging, poorer central cities and suburbs.

The report recommended:

- extraterritorial powers (for example, allow central cities to provide services like water and also to control suburban planning, zoning and development);
- intergovernmental agreements;
- voluntary metropolitan councils (of elected officials from the governments in the metro area);
- the urban county;
- transfer of functions to state government;
- metropolitan special districts (both single and multi-purpose);
- annexation;
- consolidation (of municipalities);
- city–county separation;
- city–county consolidation; and
- federation (two-tier government).

The report also discussed the strengths and weaknesses of each approach and the political feasibility of each. The approaches the Commission deemed to be more difficult to implement (and these were generally ones that required structural reform) it also ranked lower in political feasibility.

Finally, the report argued that states needed to "... unshackle the metropolitan communities so that they can have more latitude to attack the problems of the structure of local government" (85). In other words, states needed to amend their constitutions and/or adopt enabling legislation to provide local governments in metropolitan areas with the tools needed to make appropriate structural changes to address the negative externalities flowing from sprawl and fragmentation.

22 *Metropolitan Governance in America*

Roscoe C. Martin. 1963. *Metropolis in Transition: Local Government Adaptation to Changing Urban Needs*

Martin wrote this report for the US Housing and Home Finance Agency.[9] Martin noted in his introduction that the book "... was conceived as an examination by case example of the devices employed in, or at any rate available for, local government adaptation to metropolitan needs" (11). He did not, like many before him, develop a laundry list of metropolitan problems. Instead, he provided a list of a limited number of reforms that could be undertaken voluntarily by local governments to address metropolitan problems and issues.

Martin initially listed 16 possible alternatives, but actually examined only seven in brief case studies. First, here are the 16:

What he labeled *procedural adaptation*:

- informal cooperation;
- contracting;
- parallel action;
- regional councils;
- formal agreements;
- transfers of functions;
- extraterritorial jurisdiction; and
- incorporation (one could argue that incorporation is this is really structural).

What he labeled *structural adaptation*:

- annexation;
- city–county separation;
- geographical consolidation;
- functional consolidation;
- special districts;
- public authorities;
- metropolitan government; and
- the regional agency (very similar to special districts or authorities).

He followed with chapters in which he presented what he called "illustrative cases" or examples of the implementation of certain of these alternatives (12). The cases were:

- Contracting—Los Angeles County, CA (with special attention to the Lakewood plan).

---

9 The Administrator of HHFA was Robert C. Weaver, who would become the first Secretary of the US Department of Housing and Urban Development.

- Regional councils—the Mid-Willamette Valley Council of Governments (Salem OR) and Metro Washington, DC, Council of Governments.
- Planning—The Twin Cities (Minneapolis/St. Paul, MN) and Atlanta, GA.
- Special Districts—The Municipality of Metropolitan Seattle (a three-function special district).
- Functional consolidation—Adoption of a county health department in Monroe County (Rochester), NY.
- Consolidation (Nashville, Davidson County).
- A regional approach—a federal interstate compact for the Delaware Valley, involving four metro areas (Philadelphia and Allentown, PA; Trenton, NJ; and Wilmington, DE).

In his concluding chapter, Martin discussed a number of problems flowing from fragmentation, developed several hypotheses around the issue of metropolitan action (two or more governments acting in concert over a problem or issue) and called for greater state and federal action to address metropolitan problems. However, he also noted that the American system of local government was quite resilient and, no matter the problems it encountered, it would likely figure out adaptations to them, and persevere, reform or not.

Luther H. Gulick. 1966. *The Metropolitan Problem and American Ideas*

Like many of his contemporaries, Gulick accepted as an obvious truth the existence of the settlement pattern inherent in metropolitanization and the problems that came with it. "It is now recognized that the metropolitan pattern of human settlement as it has evolved on this continent is a radically new design for living and working. This I shall not argue. The proof is everywhere" (3). Gulick then argued that the growth pattern of American metro areas had produced a number of negative externalities and that the then current structural measures (or what he called governmental arrangements) did not permit them to be addressed. Among these negative externalities he included:

- poor street layout;
- lack of public transit;
- water and sewer;
- lack of reinvestment in older, declining areas;
- public health and welfare;
- public education;
- congestion;
- pollution;
- and more.

Gulick argued that the market model could not address these issues (that is, because of market failure), but he also said that the structure of local government in metro areas could not either. This was because these problems (and presumable others) were areawide and needed areawide government to address them. He then discussed "boundaries" and "local patriotism" as factors that facilitate or support strong localism, which in turn militates against areawide solutions. He strongly pushed for integration or the two-tier system. However, he also noted that most efforts to establish two-tier governments for American metropolitan areas had failed.

US Advisory Commission on Intergovernmental Relations. 1966. *Metropolitan America; Challenge to Federalism*

This report from the ACIR neatly summed up the conventional wisdom about the metropolitan problem in its preface:

> … most of the critical problems in urban areas are more in the nature of a quiet or creeping crisis. The problems that face our urban communities are too often illustrated by long term trend lines: the economic decline of central cities, the physical and social disintegration of slum areas, increasingly fragmented and overlapping patterns of government, urban sprawl, housing problems and school problems in all parts of the urban complex, inadequate transportation facilities, and growing confusion and ugliness where there should be beauty (vii).

Later in the report, the ACIR added social and economic disparities, especially suburbs versus central cities, as well as water, sewer and pollution control to the laundry list of areawide problems brought about by sprawl and fragmentation.

The report advocated solutions that were quite similar to those proposed by previous metro reformers (which, by now, are exceedingly familiar to the reader):

- extra territorial powers;
- intergovernmental agreements;
- voluntary metropolitan councils (of local government officials, not metro planning agencies);
- the urban county;
- transfers of functions to state governments;
- metropolitan special districts;
- annexation and consolidation;
- city–county separation; and
- federation or two-tier government

In the final chapter of the report, the ACIR made a number of mostly structural recommendations for state and local governments and the federal government to help achieve metro reform. Nearly all were repetitive of prior metro reform works, although one notable difference was that the report spelled out an expanded federal role in metro reform.

State and local

- home rule for all local governments;
- easier annexation;
- limits on new incorporations;
- easier creation of areawide authorities/special districts;
- easier transfers of functions from cities to counties;
- easier routes to interlocal agreements;
- extraterritorial powers;
- councils of public officials;
- metro study commissions;
- metro area planning bodies;
- establishing units in state governments for metro affairs;
- state technical and financial assistance for metro areas;
- limitations on the establishment plus oversight of special districts; and
- dispute resolution among local governments in metro areas.

Federal

- redirect federal aid to general not special purpose local governments and require better coordination of special purpose governments with their general purpose counterparts;
- encourage local governments to cooperate in metro area urban development, especially in areas that have overlapping political boundaries;
- channel federal aid for urban development through the states;
- require "… effective planning at the local level in all Federal aid programs significantly affecting urban development" (139); and
- establish federal interagency coordination for all federal aid programs affecting urban development.

Finally, the report made specific proposals for water supply and sewage disposal, recommendations for relocation of people and businesses displaced because of redevelopment, recommendations regarding social and economic disparities, and proposals to equalize local government finances.

The report recognized, however, that most reform efforts had not been successful. And it identified one of the reasons why—namely, the composition of the coalitions that supported and proposed reform. Supporters "… typically included metropolitan newspapers, Leagues of Women Voters, the central city chamber of commerce, commercial and real estate interests in the central city, radio and television stations, banks, central city officials, academic groups, manufacturing industry, utilities, and central city homeowners." Opponents "… often included farmers, rural homeowners, county employees, suburban newspapers, employees and officials of outlying local governments, and suburban commercial interests" (108). The latter group had more political clout and staying power.

Chamber of Commerce of the United States. 1967. *Modernizing Local Government*

In this update to a pamphlet of the same title published in 1960, the US Chamber of Commerce argued that local government structure was the primary reason that problems in metro areas were not being addressed. The Chamber's laundry list of metro problems included:

- traffic congestion;
- substandard housing;
- crime;
- "widespread social unrest;"[10]
- environmental pollution;
- deteriorating commercial districts; and
- lack of adequate tax structures.

The report then proposed a number of alternatives, most of which had also been proposed in prior works:

- adopt strong mayor/county executive or appointed manager form of government;
- voluntary associations of local officials;
- transfer of functions;
- contracting;
- extraterritorial powers;
- annexation;
- urban county;
- council of governments;
- state takeover of certain functions (for example, pollution control, water supply, crime labs);
- city–county consolidation;
- federated (two-tier) system;
- an areawide tax to be shared on an equalizing basis among local governments in metro areas;
- authorizing state legislation for all proposed reforms;

---

10 Note the date of the report, and its coincidence with the occurrence of riots in many American cities.

The Metropolitan Reform School 27

- a state department focusing on the problems of metro areas; and
- metro area planning bodies.

The Chamber argued that citizen apathy was the main reason that reforms had not been adopted and called on "businessmen" to step forward to help modernize local governments. Indeed, later in the report, the Chamber urged local chambers of commerce to become actively involved in efforts to reform local governments in metro areas.

US Advisory Commission on Intergovernmental Relations. 1969. *Urban America and the Federal System*

The first chapter in this report is entitled "major intergovernmental dimensions of the urban crisis," and in it the Commission presented its view of what constituted this "crisis."[11] The principal element of the urban crisis was the "fiscal and political fragmentation [of metropolitan areas] resulting in mismatch of need and resources" (1). Here, the report was referring to the increasing disparity of wealth (and hence tax base) between older central cities and their more affluent suburbs, which, in turn, produced a disparity in services. Next, the report cited the "disorderly, uneconomic and anti-social patterns of urban development and land use" (2). Here, the Commission was clearly referring to sprawl, governmental fragmentation, and suburban use of planning and zoning powers to create exclusive, mostly affluent and white enclaves beyond the borders of the central cities.

The report mainly focused on the urban fiscal crisis and made a number of recommendations to the states and the federal government concerning additional and better-coordinated aid, especially to cities and metros. The fourth chapter of the report entitled "civilizing the local government jungle," (7) made a number of essentially structural recommendations that included:

- limit new incorporations, especially of "non-viable" (84) local governments;
- enable the establishment of boundary commissions (to address changing local governmental boundaries);
- limit the creation of new special districts;
- "increase the visibility and compel intergovernmental coordination" (88); and

---

11   By the late 1960s, the term *urban crisis* was encountered frequently in any literature about cities and metropolitan areas. It became exceptionally over-used and generally meant one of two (or perhaps both) conditions: 1) the depressed fiscal condition of many older, central cities; and 2) the social unrest that had beset many of those cities.

28 *Metropolitan Governance in America*

- states should "unshackle" local governments" (89)—that is, they should amend constitutions and/or adopt enabling legislation to give local governments in metro areas more flexibility in terms of governmental structure.[12]

The report concluded by saying that repairing governmental structure was essential if the problems of the urban crisis were to be addressed. This was because the then current structure of government in metro areas stood " ... squarely in the way of efforts to marshal areawide resources to cope with areawide problems" (100).

Committee for Economic Development (CED). 1970. *Reshaping Government in Metropolitan Areas*

This report, produced by an organization headed by some of the leading business executives in the nation, described a number of the negative externalities produced by suburbanization and the fragmented governmental structure of American metropolitan areas. The negative externalities cited in the report included: education, welfare, crime, housing, jobs and training, transportation and environmental pollution.

The CED also noted the disparities in wealth between central cities and suburbs and the resulting disparities in tax revenue and public service delivery, all generally favoring the suburbs over the central cities. "... [T]he present fragmented system of government so divides the tax base that frequently resources are most scarce in those jurisdictions which have the most difficult problems. In contrast, there are some areas, particularly many suburban communities, where resources are plentiful and local problems not numerous" (24).

The CED argued that local government fragmentation in metro areas made it increasingly difficult to deal with issues both across metropolitan areas and also among local governments. It then recommended a two-tier system of government to address these problems, noting that local functions and services would remain at the local level but the metro government would be responsible for areawide functions and services.

The CED essentially repeated the conventional wisdom about "the metropolitan problem" in this report. The importance of this report was less in its substance than in the fact that a major US business organization had lent its support to the cause of metro reform. Regardless of that support, metro reform proceeded no more speedily after than before.

---

12 The specific flexibilities recommended included: transfers of functions, interlocal agreements, make annexation easier, make metro area study commissions easier to establish, regional councils, allow sub-county service and taxing districts, empower governors to resolve local disputes.

US Advisory Commission on Intergovernmental Relations. 1973–1974.
Substate Regionalism and the Federal System. **Volume I: Regional Decision Making: New Strategies for Substate Districts. October, 1973**

This was perhaps the most extensive and expansive work undertaken by the ACIR (or any other organization or author) on the issue of the metropolis and its proper governance. The report is in six volumes. I will review only the first volume because it is the only one that is directly germane to the purposes of this chapter.

Volume I is a greater than 400 pages in length document that examined the problems of metro areas and presented a number of alternatives to address them. The quotation below sets the tone and purpose of the report—the matter is now settled; it is not whether to reform metropolitan America, but how.

> Few people … are willing any longer to debate whether substate regionalism is desirable of undesirable. Regionalism is now an accepted fact of political and administrative life in both urban and rural America. The principal question is what form should substate regionalism take (6).

According to the ACIR, the culprit in metropolitan America was fragmentation and the solution was integration. The report also listed many of the usual suspect problems:

- transportation;
- housing;
- land use planning and development control;
- water supply;
- waste management (solid waste and sewage);
- air pollution;
- health planning and services;
- certain aspects of law enforcement; and
- comprehensive planning.

To this seemingly never-ending list of metro problems, the ACIR added:

- out migration of middle-class whites from central cities;
- the increasing segregation of African Americans in central cities;
- large population losses in older cities;
- lower incomes in central cities;
- lower housing values and rental prices in central cities;
- higher spending on public services by central cities;
- higher taxes in central cities; and
- central cities falling behind suburbs in employment.

30 *Metropolitan Governance in America*

This chapter then listed six alternative approaches to metro reform, including:

Structural alternatives

- special districts and authorities;
- regional councils; and
- state-mandated substate districts.

Non-structural alternatives

- A-95 review process (a mandated federal review of local government funding requests in metro areas);
- stronger federal role promoting substate regionalism; and
- stronger state role promoting substate regionalism.

Regarding at least one of these proposed reforms, special districts, the ACIR was of two minds (as were many other metro reformers). On the one hand, special districts allowed local governments in metro areas to address areawide problems. On the other hand, however, the use of special districts to do so also relieved any pressure to adopt more dramatic reforms, such as two-tier government.

> In most cases, then, considerations of political feasibility and ease of implementation (acceptance) have dictated approaches to solving areawide problems other than federation, city-county consolidation, annexation and other types of major institutional overhaul. Usually is has been more politically expedient for local decision makers to act on a function-by-function basis and establish a substate district or an independent special district, enter into an interlocal contract or joint service agreement, or cooperate in an informal voluntary manner (12).

The report went on to say, however, that these, less dramatic approaches were unsatisfactory in addressing areawide problems and noted an "… inverse relationship between effectiveness and political feasibility …" (12).

US Advisory Commission on Intergovernmental Relations. 1977.
Regionalism Revisited: Recent Areawide and Local Responses. A Brief Update of the Commission's Series of Reports on Substate Regionalism and the Federal System Published in 1973–73

This report was a brief reprise of the 1973–1976 report and suggested a three-part approach to metro reform. First, strengthen regional councils. Second, states should adopt legislation permitting the establishment of areawide governments (using a variety of techniques—for example, "… annexation, incorporation, consolidation or transfers of functions" (4)). Third, states should adopt improved policies regarding the assignment of functions to the local and metro levels.

However, perhaps the most compelling words written in the report were contained in the Chairman's Introduction. There, Chairman Robert E. Merriam noted that there had been only 25 city county consolidations in the 170 years since New Orleans and Orleans Parish merged. He also noted Metro Miami-Dade and the Twin Cities Metro Council as examples of metro governments, but then went on then to say:

> Other than these scattered examples, there has been a total resistance to the concept of even limited governmental authority to deal with urbanized problems of both metropolitan and non-metropolitan areas (1).

Despite the Chairman's observation about the difficulty in securing metro reform, the report concluded optimistically: "To sum up, the Commission believes that its three-part substate regional strategy is as relevant today as it was in 1973–74" (37).

Conclusion

The works of the metro reformers are notable for several reasons. First, there was great similarity among them in their diagnoses of the problems of metropolitan America, their prescriptions for reform and the optimism that they displayed in the face of the nearly certain defeat of their more expansive reform proposals. Additionally, and with very few exceptions, the metro reformers provided scant data or evidence to support the case for the problems identified or the suggested reforms, and most of them also largely ignored both citizen preferences and the politics of reform. Instead, the problems and solutions were self-evident and, therefore, the need for reform was crystal clear.

The works of the metro reformers, then, were largely advocacy pieces that followed a very similar pattern. First, metro areas in the US were growing and expanding without proper controls, and this uncontrolled growth was producing serious negative externalities. They then listed the externalities and proposed a variety of reforms. For the most part, the externalities identified and the reforms suggested were quite similar in work after work of the Metro Reformers.[13] Finally,

---

13   The following are among the problems most frequently cited by the Metro Reformers: uncontrolled suburban growth; sprawl; governmental fragmentation; loss of open space; traffic congestion; air and water pollution; water supply and distribution; sanitation and solid waste; public education; lack of affordable housing; disparities in wealth, tax base, services and need; segregation by race and class; disinvestment in central cities and their decline; and occasionally others. See Walker, 1987, for a listing of the typical reforms proposed. I also discuss them at length in Chapter 6.

if at all, these authors lamented that although the reforms that they suggested would be difficult to achieve, they should, in any event, be pursued.

As early as the mid-1950s, contrary voices were making themselves heard on the subject of metro reform.[14] In an article in the *Midwest Journal of Political Science*, Banfield (1957) wrote that the metro problem might well be spurious. That is, what appeared to be a problem for the metro reformers (for example, too many local governments), might instead be a boon to local residents who preferred small governments in which they had a say and which they could control.

Moreover, for various reasons, the structural solutions proposed by the reformers were unlikely to be adopted. He concluded that, at the end of the day, good old-fashioned politics would surely be needed to address metro problems. "In short, the metropolitan area problem will have to be solved—insofar as it is solved at all—by strong mayors and strong governors engaged in political give and take" (91).

Adrian (1961) went even further, calling much of the early metro reform literature "metropology ... an infantile disorder in the social sciences" (148). He criticized that literature for lacking supporting evidence, for being based on self-evident truths, for ignoring the politics, for "... unrealistic assumptions about how metropolitan areas can and should be governed," (149) for believing "... that efficiency and economy are the highest political values ...," (150) and more.

Friesema (1966) commented on "The relative academic sterility of a host of metropolitan surveys and analyses and, indeed, of municipal research in general ..." (68). This research, he further argued, was strongly reformist in nature, often lacked evidence to support its claims, and its recommendations had "... been spectacularly unsuccessful in producing reform" (69). Thus, some of the real limitations of this literature were well known, at least to social scientists fairly early on. However, neither criticism nor the failure of reform stopped the outpouring of works calling for metro reform.

Finally, when addressing whether metro reform was needed, Goodall (1968), agreeing with Adrian (1961), said that, yes, there may be fragmentation, overlap, duplication, and worse in metro areas and, that yes, to reformers this may be bad. However, to the suburban resident who wants a say in local government, having myriad local governments is a good thing, not a bad one. Goodall also noted that while the problems of metro areas could not be denied and while reforms should not, willy-nilly, be set aside, "... there are other ways than metropolitan governments for governing Metropolis" (125).

At the end of the day, at the time of the metro reformers and today, it is the expressed preferences of residents that determine the structure of local government in metropolitan areas. To quote Goodall again: "... the process of governing the American metropolis is essentially a *political* process" (234), emphasis in the

---

14 These contrary voices came mainly from political scientists. In Chapter three, I examine the take of at least one subset of economists, the Public Choice School, on the governance of metro areas.

original. It is principally through political processes that residents make their preferences known, and, since the end of the Second World War, those residents have clearly shown that they prefer fragmentation over Gargantua.

The prevailing preference set in the US today—a preference set that is at least 70 years old (85 plus, if we take Studenski as the benchmark)—is that the overwhelming majority of residents want to live in low-density residential developments, and they want myriad local governments. Furthermore, there is no reason whatsoever to think that these well-established preferences are likely to change any time in the foreseeable future. Hence, reforms of the sort proposed by the metro reformers are as unlikely to be adopted in American metropolitan areas today as they were when the Metro Reform School held sway in the urban literature.

References

Adrian, Charles R. 1961. Metropology: Folklore and field research. *Public Administration Review,* 21(3):148–157.

Banfield, Edward C. 1957. The politics of metropolitan area organization. *Midwest Journal of Political Science,* 1(1):77–91.

Chamber of Commerce of the United States. 1960. *Modernizing Local Government.* Washington, DC: Author.

Chamber of Commerce of the United States. 1967. *Modernizing Local Government.* Washington, DC: Author.

Committee for Economic Development. 1970. *Reshaping Government in Metropolitan Areas.* New York: Author.

Freisema, Paul. 1966. The metropolis and the maze of governments. *Urban Affairs Quarterly,* 2(2): 68–90.

Goodall, Leonard E. 1968. *The American Metropolis.* Columbus, OH: Charles E. Merrill.

Greer, Scott A. 1962. *Governing the Metropolis.* New York: John Wiley and Sons.

Gulick, Luther H. 1957. Metropolitan organization. *The Annals of the American Academy of Political and Social Sciences,* 314(1): 57–65.

Gulick, Luther H. 1966. *The Metropolitan Problem and American Ideas.* New York: Alfred A. Knopf.

Jones, Victor. 1942. *Metropolitan Government.* Chicago, IL: University of Chicago Press.

Martin, Roscoe C. 1963. *Metropolis in Transition: Local Government Adaptation to Changing Urban Needs.* Washington, DC: US Government Printing Office.

Studenski, Paul. 1930. *The Government of Metropolitan Areas in the United States.* New York: National Municipal League.

US Advisory Commission on Intergovernmental Relations. 1961. *Governmental Structure, Organization, and Planning in Metropolitan Areas.* Washington, DC: US Government Printing Office.

US Advisory Commission on Intergovernmental Relations. 1962. *Alternative Approaches to Governmental Reorganization in Metropolitan Areas.* Washington, DC: US Government Printing Office.

US Advisory Commission on Intergovernmental Relations. 1966. *Metropolitan America; Challenge to Federalism.* Washington, DC: US Government Printing Office.

US Advisory Commission on Intergovernmental Relations. 1969. *Urban America and the Federal System.* Washington, DC: US Government Printing Office.

US Advisory Commission on Intergovernmental Relations. 1973–1974. *Substate Regionalism and the Federal System.* Volume I: Regional Decision Making: New Strategies for Substate Districts. October, 1973. Washington, DC: US Government Printing Office.

US Advisory Commission on Intergovernmental Relations. 1977. *Regionalism Revisited: Recent Areawide and Local Responses. A Brief Update of the Commission's Series of Reports on Substate Regionalism and the Federal System Published in 1973–73.* Washington, DC: US Government Printing Office.

Walker, David. 1987. Snow White and the 17 dwarfs: From metro cooperation to governance. *National Civic Review,* 76(1):14–28.

Wood, Robert C. 1961. *1400 Governments: The Political Economy of the New York Metropolitan Region.* Cambridge, MA: Harvard University Press.

Wood, Robert C. 1957. Metropolitan government 1975: An extrapolation of trends. The new metropolis: Green belts, grass roots or Gargantua. *American Political Science Review,* 52(1): 108–122.

Wood, Robert C. 1958. *Suburbia: Its People and its Politics.* Boston, MA: Houghton Mifflin.

Chapter 3

Public Choice Theory

In this chapter, I critically examine the Public Choice theory in terms of its insights into the issue of metropolitan government and governance. I do so because, arguably for the past 50 years, Public Choice has been the major if not the only theory to contest the need for some form of areawide government or governance in metropolitan areas in the US. Indeed, and quite contrary to the positions taken by the Metropolitan Reformers and the New Regionalists, adherents to Public Choice argue that fragmented metropolitan areas function more efficiently and better serve the interests of citizens than would virtually any form of metropolitan organization.

The Tiebout Model

In my view, which I explain in due course, at best the Public Choice model is valuable because it is a thought-provoking *pure theory* about the behavior of citizens and local governments in metropolitan areas. As such it warrants attention. At worst, however, Public Choice is a woefully inadequate description of the reality of the behavior of citizens and local governments in these areas. Public Choice misleads those who are concerned about the problems and issues that face entire metropolitan areas, and it distracts from a more nuanced and, in the end, a more correct understanding of behavior in and likely solutions to the problems of those areas.

At its simplest, Public Choice theory first posits the existence of numerous local governments in the fragmented polycentric metropolis area and then argues that this array of governments provides citizens with the option to choose among them the residential location that best suits their (the citizens') preferences for packages of services and taxes. Thus, the fragmented metropolis functions in a manner that is analogous to the workings of the market in a free market economy. The theory also posits that each of the multiple local governments in a metropolitan area acts in a manner similar to that of firms competing in the market, offering distinct goods or services to prospective consumers. Indeed, local governments offer distinct packages of taxes and services, and citizens then decide among these different packages their preferred residential locations.

For a market example, think about the numerous automobile dealerships in a metropolitan area, each with its brand of automobile, different models, sizes, colors, styles, accoutrements, reliability, value and, of course, price, to name a few of the characteristics that consumers might consider when buying a car. Think also of the numerous car buyers, each with his or her distinct set of preferences and his or her individual wallet. Just as these customers choose cars from the range of offerings available at the multiple dealerships, and do so based on their own individual preferences, so according to the Public Choice theory do citizens ("consumer–voters" in the Public Choice vocabulary) when choosing their places of residence. That is, citizens' preferences for a particular set or package of services and taxes will lead them to move ("vote with their feet" in the Public Choice vocabulary) to the local government that most closely approximates their preferences. Or so say the Public Choice theorists.

Perhaps the single most important figure in the history of Public Choice theory, at least as applied to metropolitan government and governance, is Charles Tiebout. In his 1956 article titled "A Pure Theory of Local Expenditures," Tiebout used economic reasoning to establish a model of the fragmented or polycentric metropolis to show that it is a quasi-market mechanism offering different alternatives to citizens to choose where to live based on the package of taxes and services that each local government in the metropolitan area offers. This model became the foundation of the Public Choice thinking and analysis around the subject of metropolitan government and governance.

Tiebout's is a "pure theory," as he labeled it in the title of the paper. As a pure theory, Tiebout made several extreme assumptions—assumptions that he recognized did not exist in the real world. However, Tiebout (and others since him) have argued that, for the purpose of theorizing, the assumptions are justifiable. Here, I differ from Tiebout and his followers. For the purpose of theorizing, extreme assumptions may be justifiable, but when using a theory or model to explain and predict behavior, assumptions take on a different and more important meaning. To be useful, except in the narrowest academic sense, assumptions must be grounded and must accurately reflect the objective reality around them. I argue that the utility of the Tiebout model in the real world is considerably limited by its assumptions, an issue to which I turn presently.

First, I list (and directly quote) the seven assumptions in the model (p. 419).

1. Consumer-voters are fully mobile and will move to that community where their preference patterns, which are set, are best satisfied.
2. Consumer-voters are assumed to have full knowledge of differences among revenue and expenditure patterns and to react to these differences.
3. There are a large number of communities in which the consumer-voters may choose to live.
4. Restrictions due to employment opportunities are not considered. It may be assumed that all persons are living on dividend income.
5. The public services supplied exhibit no external economies or diseconomies between communities.
6. For every pattern of community services ... there is an optimal community size. This optimum is defined in terms of the number of residents for which this bundle of services can be produced at the lowest average cost ...

7. The last assumption is that communities below the optimum size seek to attract new residents to lower average costs. Those above optimum size do just the opposite. Those at an optimum try to keep their populations constant.

Next, I explain and evaluate these assumptions and consider their effects on the real world utility of the model. The Public Choice literature, insofar as it addresses metropolitan governance, is largely shaped around these assumptions and their implications. That literature is huge and much of it is devoted to attempting to show that the model accurately explains and predicts the behavior of citizens and local governments in metropolitan areas (mostly in the US).[1] In my view, however, the model and its application are only as good as the underlying assumptions, which I will show in the following pages are considerably challenged.

Assumption 1: Full mobility and sorting

Tiebout's first assumption is that citizens will choose where to live based upon the package of taxes and services that local governments provide, seeking the package that most closely fits their preferences. Citizens will "vote with their feet" to get there. That is, they will move from a local government that fails to satisfy their preferences to one that does satisfy them.

This assumption has three parts. First, citizens are fully mobile. There are no limitations whatsoever on their ability to move. Second, citizens' preferences for a package of taxes and services are immutable and unchanging. Third, citizens will move to where their preferences send them (in other words, they will act rationally in an economic sense with regard to residential location).

There is a significant problem with the idea that citizens are perfectly mobile. In reality, they are not. In their decisions about residential location, citizens' choices are always constrained in some way or ways (for example, Stephens and Wikstron, 2000). Substantial disparities exist between those who can move and those who cannot. Some, mainly the very wealthy, may be able to move with greater ease (indeed, with seemingly no limitations at all) than, say, the poor. But even affluent and certainly middle-class families, to say nothing of the poor, experience considerable constraints on their ability to move from one location to another.

Moreover, not all limitations are financial. Kay and Marsh (2007) have noted that "The residential mobility literature appears to present the Tiebout Model with a problem" (175). This is because, among other things, the issue of the tax-service packages of local governments as a reason why people move is either not found in this literature or is only peripheral to decisions to move (Kay and Marsh,

---

1 For a brief but excellent summary of some of the major contributions to that literature, see G. Ross Stephens and Nelson Wikstrom, 2000, *Metropolitan Government and Governance: Theoretical Perspectives, Empirical Analysis and the Future*. New York: Oxford University Press.

2007). Additionally, many factors beyond tax-services packages affect citizens' residential location decisions (for example, Boheikm and Taylor, 2002; Bembry and Norris, 2005; Boadway and Tremblay, 2011).

According to the mobility literature, regional home price differentials and zoning regulations also restrict free mobility (Sharp, 1984; Boheikm and Taylor, 2002). And these restrictions do not affect all income and racial groups equally. "Exclusionary zoning regulations enacted by suburbs can limit housing availability and drive up the price of accommodations. For racial minorities, the poor, and even for younger workers and newly marrieds, actions of various governments in the polycentric metropolis may restrict housing choice" (Ross and Levine, 1996: p. 337).

Historically, African–Americans have faced greater limitations on their residential mobility than other groups due to segregation and discrimination (Shumaker and Stokols, 1982; Clark, 1992; South and Deane, 1993; South and Crowder, 1997; Bembry and Norris, 2005). Local land use regulations and zoning practices have been designed, especially in the suburbs, to keep the local communities segregated by race and class (Rossi and Shlay, 1982; Bembry and Norris, 2005).

For all of these reasons, and perhaps more, full mobility does not and almost certainly cannot exist.

The second part of Tiebout's mobility and sorting assumption is that citizens' preference patterns are set and unchanging; they are fixed. In reality, people generally do not have set of immutable preferences. Some scholars argue that preferences are constructed and change according to different environmental settings (for example, Lichtenstein and Slavic, 2006; Hill, 2008). The residential mobility literature also tells us that preferences change with one's life situation. The young have different housing preferences, for example, than middle-aged persons with families and older empty nesters. And changing family circumstances (for example, children v. no children, a family's financial status, and so on) affect housing preferences (Kay and Marsh, 2005).

Additionally, there is strong evidence from Stein's study (1987) that examined data from over 11,000 municipalities in 224 metropolitan areas that citizens' preferences for public services are rather homogeneous, at least concerning basic services such as police, fire and sanitation. "People rarely concern themselves with the manner in which these basic functions are performed" (152). In the same paper, Stein also found that, while sorting occurred, there was no relationship between sorting and a range of independent variables, except race.

Therefore, the assumption that citizens have set and ranked order preferences for specific tax-service packages does not accurately represent the complexity of preference construction and the mobility decision process. Indeed, as Hill (2008) has noted (citing von Weiszaker, 2005), this assumption has been accepted within the social sciences by neoclassical economics only and no one else.

Even if I assume that preferences are set, whether citizens behave according to these preferences is a different matter. In other words, will people behave in an economically rational matter with respect to their preferences? According to rational choice theory, people choose the best alternatives according to their preferences in order to maximize their utilities. However, according to bounded rationality theory, limitations of information, time, and cognitive abilities restrict the rationality of individuals. Because of these limitations, individuals can only make simplified comparisons between alternatives and make satisficing decisions rather than optimal ones.[2]

Bembry and Norris (2005) explained bounded rationality in the context of the mobility decisions of the poor, showing both information and cognitive limitations:

> The poor often have little or no direct experience with nonpoor neighborhoods and the private housing market, and have little contact with people who can give them accurate information about them. Therefore, their mobility decisions are made through distorted filters, which limits their choices, and renders their search process ineffective. Thus, through a combination of political/structural factors and socio-cultural influences, the poor, when they do make mobility decisions, often find themselves in impoverished neighborhoods much like the ones they left (97).

Some scholars argue that even if there were no restrictions on or cost to mobility, some people would prefer to stay in their communities and try to fight and change the system instead of exiting (Neenan and Ethridge, 1984; Lowery and Lyons, 1989). Voting with their feet may not be the most prevalent way by which people find a way to get their public goods preferences met. Since moving costs can be quite high (financially and otherwise), some people may find it more desirable to get their local governments to change policies and practices (for example, taxes and services) through the political process (for example, political activism including assembly, petition, lobbying, seeking office, and so on) than to move to different communities.

Lowery and Lyons (1989) have noted that residents may not be attentive to the tax-service bundles of their local governments even if they are not happy with them because they may think that a higher level of government is more important in their daily lives and tax-service bundles. This argument is also related to Tiebout's second assumption (perfect information), which I discuss later. Lowery and Lyons argued that if Tiebout's sorting hypothesis is valid, then there would be very little exit due to dissatisfaction because the communities would initially have been formed by the people who prefer a particular tax-service bundle. This would have attracted like-minded persons. And, the combination of initial and later residents with the same preferences would keep the tax-service bundle from changing.

Then there is the broader question of why people move and whether the reasons are consistent with this Tiebout assumption. Kay and Marsh (2007) reviewed the

---

2   Herbert Simon (1956). Satisficing means to make decisions that satisfy and suffice, not optimize.

40   *Metropolitan Governance in America*

residential mobility literature starting with Rossi's (1955) book *Why Families Move*. Rossi found that an important fraction of moves included those that were "forced," such as involuntary moves, evictions, moves related to marriage, divorce or unemployment. More recent studies by Ermisch and Di Salvo (1996) and Kan (1999) confirm Rossi's finding of the importance of unanticipated events on mobility. Housing quality and price are also important determinants of residents' decisions about where to live (Sharp, 1984). And in their in-depth study, Dowding et al. (1994) found that the literature provided only "… mixed evidence that local tax and expenditure variables affect this [sorting] process" (715).

In sum, Tiebout's first assumption is unrealistic, empirically challenged and almost completely inconsistent with the way people actually behave. People are not fully mobile. They do not have immutable preferences on tax-service packages of local governments (or probably anything else). They do not behave in an economically rational manner when making housing location decisions. And, they do not move principally, if at all, because of the tax-service packages that local governments offer.

Assumption 2: Perfect information and rationality

The model's second assumption is that people have complete knowledge about the tax-service packages of the local governments in their metropolitan areas and that they behave rationally in relation to that knowledge. That is, individuals choose to live in communities in which the tax-service package most closely meets their preferences. The major flaws in this assumption are, first, the claim about full knowledge; second, the notion that people will act as if they were *homo economicus* with that information and move accordingly; and, third, the implicit assumption that local tax-service packages do not change.

Because of cognitive and other limitations (for example, time, money, education, motivation), human beings rarely, if ever, have full knowledge or even something approximating full knowledge about anything. Even if achieving something close to full knowledge were possible about some things, in the fragmented metropolis, with its tens and sometimes hundreds of governments, it would be impossible for anyone to know the tax-service packages of all of the governments. And research has shown that in the real world people simply do not have full information of the tax-service packages of local governments in their regions (Lowery and Lyons, 1989).

The response from the Public Choice school to this criticism is that although people do not have full knowledge, they use rules of thumb and a variety of other techniques to become as informed as they feel they need to be, and that they then act accordingly. In other words, they act in a boundedly rational manner (Simon, 1957). While undoubtedly true, this response does not rescue the assumption of full knowledge. Nor can it demonstrate that consumer voters actually seek residential location based solely or primarily on their preferences for tax-service packages. As I previously noted, the mobility literature strongly suggests that this is largely,

Public Choice Theory 41

if not exclusively, not the case. That literature shows that the decision to move is a complex one in which the tax-service package of local governments hardly appears as an explanatory variable, and when it does it is peripheral to other, more important factors that affect the decision to move (Kay and Marsh, 2007; Lowery and Lyons, 1989).

Of course, even Tiebout admitted the weaknesses of assumptions one and two:

> Assumptions 1 and 2 should be checked against reality. Consumer-voters do not have perfect knowledge and set preferences, nor are they perfectly mobile (423).

Assumption 3: Many local governments from which to choose

The model's third assumption is that numerous local governments exist from which the consumer–voter can select the one that best fits his or her preferences. Certainly, in most of the larger metropolitan areas in the US, this assumption comes reasonably close to reality because those metropolitan areas do, indeed, contain numerous local governments.[3] However, in at least one large metropolitan area, Baltimore (the 18th largest in the US in 2010), there is not a surfeit of local governments. There is one large municipality (Baltimore), five county governments (two of which have no municipalities), and only 13 other municipalities, all of which are small in geography and population. Moreover, in smaller American metropolitan areas (of which there are many), the number of governments from which to choose is not always great.[4] Here again, the model's assumption is empirically challenged.

Several other problems exist with this assumption. The sheer number of communities must be nearly infinite in order to ensure that each consumer–voter is able to find one that meets his or her preferences. The existence of such a number of local governments is simply not realistic, nor legally or politically possible. Next, each of these governments would have to have the administrative, political and financial wherewithal to create a tax-service package to attract a particular set of residents. I know that metropolitan areas contain local governments that are resource rich and resource poor and many in between. Most local governments are small, and small as well as poor governments do not have the financial capacity to offer attractive tax-service packages.[5] And, they are unlikely to possess the administrative and political ability to craft and implement such policies.

---

3   In 2010, the average number of general-purpose local governments per metropolitan area in the US was 102. Of course, some had far more and some far less.

4   Of the 381 metro areas in the US in 2010, only 102 had populations greater than 500,000.

5   According to the International City/County Management Association (ICMA), of the 7,506 general-purpose local governments with populations greater than 2,500 in the US in 2000, 6,049 (80 percent) had 10,000 or fewer residents.

Implicit in this assumption also is the view that with a large number of local governments a great variation in the tax-service packages will exist in metropolitan areas. Thus, each resident would be able to find a community that meets his or her preferences. Oates (1969) has argued that different tax rates among communities can be considered as evidence supporting the Tiebout model. However, Ladd (1992) has shown that there is tax mimicking among neighboring counties in metropolitan areas. It is also not unusual for local governments (particularly those that are neighbors) to exhibit considerable similarity in governmental structure and service provision, although service quality may differ. This being the case—that is, greater similarity than difference among many local governments in a region—there would be much less incentive for consumer–voters to move, if in fact they moved for this reason to begin with.

Finally, a greater number of governments produces greater complexity and lack of transparency. The fragmented metropolis " … results in a bewildering maze of service arrangements incomprehensible to the average voter. This condition serves to undermine accountability to the citizens and local democracy" (Stephens and Wikstrom, 2000: p. 120).

Assumption 4: Everyone lives on dividend income

The fourth assumption is that no one is gainfully employed and that everyone lives on dividend income. This is so clearly false that I should need to go no further to address it. Very few persons actually live solely or even principally on dividend or other unearned income. Work in some form is the most important source of income for nearly all non-retired Americans. As a result, residential location is often influenced, at least in part, by the location of one's employment. This is true even though some fraction of employed persons is almost always willing to accept long commutes between their residences and their places of work.

The trend of moving to where one works is supported by the literature. Job-related moves constitute a substantial proportion of voluntary moves. These moves are usually facilitated by the unemployed, who go somewhere else to seek or take a job, and professional workers, who have access to relocation expenses (Kay and Marsh, 2007). This leads these two groups, more than anyone else, to migrate voluntarily within and among regions due to factors having little or nothing to do with local government tax-service packages.

Assumption 5: No externalities and no diseconomies

The fifth assumption is that there are no spillovers (externalities) and no economies of scale to be found in metropolitan areas. Once again the assumption is not empirically accurate. The principal negative externalities that urban scholarship has identified over the past 50 plus years include at least the following: uncontrolled suburban growth; sprawl; governmental fragmentation; loss of open space; traffic congestion; air and water pollution; water supply and distribution; sanitation and solid waste; public education; lack of affordable housing; disparities in wealth, tax base, services and need; segregation by race and class; disinvestment in central cities and their decline; and occasionally others. Moreover, the costs of these externalities are unevenly distributed across metropolitan areas, often with poorer jurisdictions shouldering disproportionately higher costs relative to their fiscal capacity.

The failure to recognize and to address negative externalities is yet another significant weakness of the Tiebout model and of Public Choice theory in general. Addressing negative externalities was, as I showed in Chapter 2, among the most compelling reasons for the structural reforms that the Metropolitan Reformers proposed. It is one of the main reasons that the New Regionalists (Chapter 4) call for governance solutions in metropolitan areas.

Policies that deal with spillovers, especially policies that are redistributive, are hard or impossible for local jurisdictions in metropolitan areas to adopt. This is because such policies would require jurisdictions either to give up scarce resources (that is, tax dollars) or to surrender some of their autonomy, and they are loath to do either (Norris, 2001). Indeed, for mostly political reasons, local governments in metropolitan areas have historically shown little or no willingness to cooperate with one another to address these externalities (Norris, 2001; Howell-Moroney, 2008). This, then, makes the failure of the pubic choice school to address externalities even more serious.

In addition to externalities, many diseconomies of scale occur as a result of a metropolitan area sprawling outward, making it more difficult and more costly, for example, to build and maintain infrastructure (Ross and Levine, 1996). In the polycentric metropolitan area, the existence of numerous local governments also means that there will be considerable duplication—seemingly every local government, regardless of size or fiscal capacity, having its own police department, fire department, municipal administration and so forth. These local governments, operating as separate entities, may also fail to take advantage of opportunities for economies of scale. A good example of this is in the area of purchasing, where larger governments having greater financial "throw weight" can negotiate better deals with vendors for goods and services than can smaller ones. There certainly are other examples in many functional areas.

Another important limitation of polycentrism, and hence of Public Choice theory, is that it "tends to exacerbate parochialism" (Ross and Levine, 1996: p. 337). Keating has observed that the fragmented metropolitan area " ... produces a parochial leadership and defines the policy agenda in narrow terms" (126). Here, local governments are free to do whatever is in their own economic self-interests, often acting to the detriment of their neighbors and of the overall region. They act with little or no concern about negative consequences (spillovers) from their actions and rarely engage in cooperative endeavors except when it suits their own needs. Hence, externalities such as those I listed above are rarely addressed on a regional level (see also Ross and Levine, 1996; Norris, 2001; Howell-Moroney, 2008).

44   *Metropolitan Governance in America*

Finally, I note that Tiebout recognized that externalities do exist. "There are obvious external economies and diseconomies between communities" (423). Indeed, he went on to say that if the externalities are severe enough, "some form of integration may be indicated" (423). Nevertheless, in most of the pubic choice literature, the assumption is that externalities do not exist and if they do it is the job of higher levels of government to address them.

Assumption 6: Optimal community size

Tiebout's sixth assumption is that there is an optimal community size and that the optimum is the number of residents for whom services can be provided the most efficiently. Thus, there is an ideal state or equilibrium to be achieved between all members of a community defined by the size of said community that is optimal for allocation of resources. Clearly this assumption is a false. Nowhere in the country (or world, for that matter) is there an optimal size for a local government. Were there, I would not observe the great variation in local government sizes—in the US, from tiny places with fewer than 100 residents to New York City (8.34 million residents in 2012).

To compound matters, later in the article Tiebout wrote: "There is no reason why the number of communities will not be equal to the population" (421). This would suggest that perfect efficiency would be met if there were one government (a package of taxes and services) for each resident (a set of preferences). This might be efficient from the standpoint of each resident achieving his or her desired outcome in terms of taxes and services, but it is impractical, legally and politically impossible and would produce utter chaos.

Assumption 7: Communities keep their optimum size

The model's final assumption is that communities below the optimum size will endeavor to add residents while those at an optimum will endeavor not to lose population. Communities over the optimum, however, would not evict residents, but "economic forces are at work to push people out … " (Tiebout, 1956, p 420).

In reality, only local governments that are very well-off fiscally or those that are "built out" try to discourage further population growth. Nearly all others, by contrast, seek more residents. And, nearly all local governments seek more economic growth in order to provide more jobs for residents and to enhance the local tax base (Peterson, 1981). This behavior by local governments has little to do with efficiency of service delivery and much to do with the fiscal structure of local government in the US.

On average, American local governments rely very little on the federal government and considerably more on their state governments for funding. For example, of intergovernmental revenue received by local governments in 2011, about 13 percent came from the federal government versus 87 percent from the states, although this varies by state and among local governments. Local governments rely substantially more on locally derived revenue, especially from the property tax. On average, own source revenue in 2011 accounted for 62 percent of local government funding (versus 32 percent intergovernmental revenue). About 64 percent of local revenue came from local taxes and, of that, 74 percent was produced by the local property tax (Barnett and Vidal, 2013). Again, this varies by state and among local governments.

In order to have sufficient funds to support the local budget, therefore, a local government must have an adequate tax base. This almost inevitably means that a local government must continue to grow economically, if not in terms of population as well. If it does not grow, it will stagnate or decline and will not be able to pay its bills.

Many factors influence whether a local government's population increases, is stable or decreases. Some are general in nature, while others are more specific to particular local governments. For example, weather is a factor—communities in the Sunbelt have long been growing while those in the Frostbelt have experienced slow growth or outright decline. Of course, other factors have influenced this population shift as well, such as the decline in manufacturing in at least the northeastern and midwestern states. Many central cities in the northeast and midwest have also seen great population loss and substantial change in population composition due to the combined effects of the Great Migration and white flight. Some cities are seen as desirable locations (for example, Boston, MA and San Francisco, CA) while others not so much (for example, Camden, NJ and Gary, IN). And, then, there are the fairly standard push and pull factors that urban scholars have documented over the years that influence a locale's population ebb and flow

Need I mention Detroit, Michigan circa 2013? In 1950, Detroit had a population of about 1.85 million. Forty years later in 1990, its population was just over one million—having lost nearly 800,000 residents in that period (an average of 20,000 per year, 200,000 per decade). Between 1990 and 2012, Detroit lost another 350,000 residents. During this 60-plus year period, Detroit did virtually nothing to attract population and much to repel residents. (As a result of population loss as well as other factors, Detroit's fiscal situation became so bad that in 2013 the Governor of Michigan appointed a fiscal manager for the city who, in short order, declared the city bankrupt.)

For these and other reasons, it is hard to imagine that an optimum size exists for local governments, or if it does exist, how it might be achieved in the real world or, if achieved, how it might be sustained. Furthermore, any assumption about optimal local government size, what local governments will or will not do regarding population gain or loss should be informed by empirical investigation rather than speculation.

Tiebout Expanded

Five years after Tiebout published "A pure theory of local expenditures," an article by Vincent Ostrom, Charles Tiebout and Robert Warren (1961), entitled "The organization of government in metropolitan areas: A theoretical inquiry," appeared in the *American Political Science Review*. Among other things, the article expanded on "A pure theory" and also directly attacked one of the main premises of the Metropolitan Reformers. That premise, as I showed in Chapter 2, is that the polycentric metropolitan area is incapable of addressing satisfactorily, if at all, the many, serious negative externalities that occur as the result of the governmental fragmentation inherent in polycentrism.

In their 1961 article, Ostrom et al. claimed just the opposite—the polycentric metropolitan area was superior to that called "Gargantua" (areawide government). They argued that the Metropolitan Reformers got it wrong when the latter claimed that:

> ... the people of a metropolitan region have no general instrumentality of government available to deal directly with the range of problems which they share in common (831).

The Metropolitan reformers were also wrong because of their view that:

> Autonomous units of government, acting in their own behalf, are considered incapable of resolving the diverse problems of the wider metropolitan community (831).

In the remainder of the article, Ostrom et al. addressed whether and how local governments in metropolitan areas cooperate with one another to address certain issues. However, they confined their analysis to the production and provision of public goods while ignoring other functions of and services provided by local governments and the control of negative externalities. Plenty of evidence was available in 1961 (and plenty is available at this writing) that local governments do, indeed, cooperate. So, there was little new or striking in that observation.

In their article, Ostrom et al. used the Lakewood Plan as a good example of interlocal cooperation to deliver services. They argued that under the Lakewood Plan:[6]

> A polycentric political system can be viable in supplying a variety of public goods with many different scales of organization and in providing optimal arrangements for the production and consumption of public goods (839).

I agree that the Lakewood Plan and numerous of other methods (for example, contracting out, interlocal agreements, and so on) represent cooperative approaches that local governments can and do take to deliver public goods and services.

---

6 The Lakewood Plan is a method of contracting out for city services. At the time it was created (1954) it was considered quite innovative. See the City of Lakewood website for a description. http://www.lakewoodcity.org/about_lakewood/community_profile/the_ lakewood_plan.asp.

Public Choice Theory   47

However, the operative words here are *goods and services*. Such methods are rarely used to control negative externalities such as those with which the Metropolitan Reformers were and the New Regionalists are so concerned.

At the same time, however, that Ostrom et al. said that polycentrism works, they undermined their own argument in three important ways. First, they agreed with the Metropolitan Reformers that Gargantua (areawide government) might be appropriate under certain circumstances, that is, to address areawide problems.

> Gargantua unquestionably provides the appropriate scale of organization for many huge public services ... By definition, gargantua should be best able to deal with metropolitan wide problems at the metropolitan level (837).

Although they then proceeded to criticize Gargantua for having a "complex hierarchical or bureaucratic structure," imposing excessive cost, and being "insensitive and clumsy" (without, I might note, any evidence), they nevertheless concluded that metropolitan-wide organization remains appropriate "for a limited number of public services ..." (837–838).

Second, Ostrom et al. contradicted their earlier position that local governments in metropolitan areas are willing to cooperate to address negative externalities when they recognized that local governments have little incentive to take on the costs of "... adverse consequences which are shared by a wider public." (840). This negates their criticism earlier in the article of the Metropolitan Reformers' argument that makes this exact point for this exact reason. Local governments do not cooperate on matters that threaten their autonomy and when they do cooperate it is more likely than not over what Oliver Williams (1967) called systems maintenance rather than lifestyle issues (see Chapter 5).

And, finally, when discussing how local governments should address areawide problems (they call these "conflicts"), Ostrom et al. briefly mentioned (a bit over one page in a 12-page article) only three alternatives: 1) recourse to the courts; 2) the creation of special districts; and 3) invoking higher levels of government. Regarding the latter, they were not keen at all because doing so would undermine local autonomy.

If I ignore the contradictions in this paper, the message that one takes from it (and the message Ostrom et al. clearly intended), is that the local governments in the polycentric metropolitan area are capable of cooperating and do cooperate in the provision of public goods (no argument from me) and that no over-arching government is needed (a major argument from at least the Metropolitan Reformers).

My view here is similar to that of the Metropolitan Reformers and the New Regionalists. Simply put, several, very serious negative externalities exist in the polycentric metropolitan areas, and local governments, if left to their own devices, either cannot or will not address them. Therefore, some other instrumentality or instrumentalities are needed if they are to be addressed at all. I return to this subject later in the book. For now I turn to an examination of the normative aspects of the Tiebout model (as extended by Ostrom, Tiebout and Warren).

Normative Aspects of the Model

According to Howell-Moroney, Tiebout did not make normative claims in his seminal article. However, "Subsequent scholarship has made very strong normative claims ..." (98). Indeed, the Public Choice literature that has followed the Tiebout model includes a number of normative elements, the principal one of which is that the fragmented or polycentric metropolis is superior to any alternative way of organizing governments in metropolitan areas. Others include: a focus on pubic goods and services; economics trumps all other values (for example equity); localism is better; smaller governments are better; more governments are better; and competition among local governments is good. The Public Choice literature also fails to take politics into account when addressing the organizational arrangement of governments in metropolitan areas.

Perhaps its greatest contribution to the regionalism debate has been the model's insistence that polycentrism is better than Gargantua. However, as I have noted, Tiebout himself, as well as others who have followed him, have agreed that under some circumstances areawide government would be appropriate. Yet, Tiebout severely restricted the basis on which areawide government would be justified. "Municipal integration is justified only if more of the same service is forthcoming at the same total cost and without reduction of any other service" (423).

Prior to the Tiebout model, the predominant view among scholars, practitioners and observers of metropolitan affairs was that metropolitan areas consisted of crazy quilt patterns of often overlapping and duplicative governments that were difficult for local citizens to understand, and those governments were incapable of managing important areawide problems and issues. Since the Tiebout model, the debate has widened and now has two distinct sides—one that favors some form of metropolitan governance over at least some issues and one that says that none is needed.

The Public Choice insistence that polycentrism is superior is normative because it is motivated by a two, equally normative, beliefs (and I stress *beliefs* here)—namely that citizens should be totally free to live wherever they want (regardless of the consequences) and that efficiency is the principal (if not the sole) value by which to judge local government. While I agree that freedom is not only a good thing but is essential to democracy and human development, freedom is hardly ever absolute. This includes the freedom to choose where to live. For example, in most communities, people cannot establish residences in areas zoned for commercial or industrial use, in public parks and on environmentally sensitive lands, to name a few restrictions. People are not free to move wherever they want for other reasons as well, including the limitations I discussed earlier in this chapter.

I also agree that efficiency is an important value by which to judge governmental performance. However, efficiency is not the sole or even always the primary value by which to judge local governments. Here, I have in mind such other values as effectiveness, equity, legality, environmental protection and process values. Each of these values plays a role in public policy outcomes for and among local governments. And, at different times one or more of these values will almost certainly be the most important one in determining a public policy outcome. Efficiency, whether defined as *Pareto optimality* or as achieving the greatest output for the fewest inputs, therefore, is not and should not be the most important (certainly not the sole) value by which to evaluate local governments or the governance of metropolitan areas.

Yet, in the Public Choice world, efficiency trumps all other values. The Tiebout model's and subsequent Public Choice scholars' main concern is whether the organization of the metropolitan area is economically efficient or not. This is not solely a concern with the cost of service delivery (is it more or less costly for a dozen or 100 individual local governments or an areawide government to provide police service?) but also whether it is more efficient for consumer–voters to achieve their goal of finding a residential location that most closely meets their preferences. Values like fairness and equity, effectiveness, environmental protection and others have no place in Public Choice world. For example, Tiebout claimed that "... municipal integration is justified only if more of any service is forthcoming at the same total cost and without reduction of any other service" (423). I and many other scholars would argue that there are other equally valid reasons than cost and efficiency to consider areawide government. Efficiency is not the only value that motivates or should motivate public policy and the organization of governments in metropolitan areas.

As Howell-Moroney has said, if metropolitan problems were limited to matters of service efficiency:

> ... Public Choice would have been successful in settling most of my questions about the best way to approach metropolitan governance. But polycentric systems are inextricably linked to a whole set of other problems stemming from the municipal boundaries that polycentric systems leave intact (100).

Even followers of Tiebout concur that the efficiency value is challenged. Buchanan and Goetz (1972) have argued that "Local governmental units do not, and cannot, behave in the manner that the efficiency criterion would dictate" (38).

A third normative feature is the model's exclusive focus on pubic goods and services. "I view the business of government in metropolitan areas as providing 'public goods and services'" (Ostrom et al., 1961: p. 832). However, in reality, the job of government is much more than just to provide public goods and services. To give but one example, the preamble to the US constitution lists six functions of the federal government: form a more perfect union, establish justice, provide for the common defense, secure the blessings of liberty, promote the general welfare, and insure domestic tranquility. These, clearly, are broad purposes and, equally clearly, they involve far more than simply the provision of public goods. And both state and local governments in the US are involved in each of these functional areas.

Thus, it is highly prejudicial to restrict any analysis of the affairs of metropolitan areas solely to the provision of what are essentially consumer goods. Doing so almost certainly ensures that the outcome of the analysis will favor the provision of such goods over other governmental functions and efficiency over other values.

Fourth, localism is better. That is, government closest to the people is the best. Since at least the days of Thomas Jefferson, this has been the dominant American view of government, even though in this country there are also large municipalities, large counties (those with either large land areas or large populations or both), state governments and, of course, the federal government. All of these governments have a place in intergovernmental schema of the United States. Thus localism is not always, *ipso facto*, better.

Moreover, to understand whether one schema is "better," one would have to ask, what is meant by better? Better at what, under what circumstances, during what time period, and so on? Does anyone really believe that local governments that are underfunded, incompetent, corrupt, that discriminate against any portion of their citizenry are "better" in any meaningful sense? Do not and should not state governments and the federal government step in from time to time to reign in abuses by local governments?

Thus, I conclude that local governments may or may not be better than higher levels of government, including structures of metropolitan government, at least under some circumstances and for certain tasks. In any event this is an empirical question. It is not something that can be known a priori, unless it is normative, a matter of preference, a bias.

In addition, according to some scholars, localism itself produces an undesirable (for the whole metropolitan area) outcome—parochialism—that makes impossible the adoption of a broader view of the good of the entire area: "... [S]cholars studying spillovers [have] taught us that municipal boundaries augment a localized and myopic sense of citizen responsibility, dampening any concern for any area but one's own" (Howell-Moroney, 2008: p. 104).

Fifth, smaller governments are better. This is related to but somewhat different from localism is better. Many local governments in US metropolitan areas are small (as measured by population) and a non-trivial fraction of these (as well as a number of larger governments) seem always to be on the verge of/or actually in financial trouble because they cannot provide sufficient tax bases to meet the needs of the residents. The smallest of governments are sometimes referred to as "toy governments" because they encompass small areas, have small populations, have few elected officials, little or no staff and provide few or no services directly. No one can seriously believe that such governments are better (compared to what?). Moreover, by nearly any measure some large governments work well while some small governments do not. In any event, size and the ability to function well is an empirical question.

Sixth, more governments are better. Here, too, the focus is on population. As Tiebout indicated, perfect efficiency would be met if there were one government for each resident. For a variety of reasons, this cannot happen, but the belief continues to exist among Public Choice advocates that more governments means more choice for citizens in their search for a place to live that meets their preferences.

As I indicated earlier, citizens' choices are limited in a number of ways. Merely having more governments does not necessarily improve those choices.

Seventh, in the Public Choice world, competition among local governments is good because it would make laggard governments improve their tax-service packages. This, too, is an empirical question. Does competition among local governments exist in metropolitan areas? What forms of competition? Under what circumstances? According to Dowding et al. (1994), hardly any credible evidence exists to support the conclusion that more governments produce more competition.

There is ample scholarly literature that shows that local governments do compete—but mainly for business and economic development in order to enhance their tax bases. There is little or no literature that shows that they directly or consciously compete for residents. Yes, most local governments want to attract residents and residents of a certain type (those with resource surplus, not resource needs). Local governments may also adopt policies and take actions to make sure that their communities are and remain attractive to existing and potential residents. But desiring to attract residents and taking actions to keep the community attractive are different from engaging in competition with other governments to attract residents.

Moreover, there is the question of whether the alleged competition produces the hypothesized effect of making laggard governments improve themselves. Here, I am unaware of any studies that examine this question. However, there is ample anecdotal evidence to suggest that the answer is no. May I again cite Detroit and the many cities like it in the US that have been in decline for many years and do not seem to be capable of doing anything to improve their competitive position? Moreover, those local governments that have suffered severe decline and have been at least somewhat successful in halting or reversing this course (for example, Boston, MA) have not been driven to do so because competition from their suburbs but rather for their very survival.

Finally, there is the model's normative preference is for a world in which economic thinking and behavior are paramount. Local governments act rationally to create packages of taxes and services in order to attract certain types of residents; consumer–voters have fixed preferences for patterns of taxes and services, and they act rationally (in an economic sense) on those preferences to move to communities where the packages of taxes and services most closely meet their preferences.

As I have shown, the reality is that decisions regarding where people choose to live are much more nuanced and complex than a singular focus on the tax-service package. But more importantly for the point I am making here, it is largely politics, not economics that determines the shape of a metropolitan area and its governments and its governance (Norris, 2001). A model that neglects the political dimension shows both a clear bias and a clear preference for a state of affairs that does not, probably cannot, exist and, in my opinion, probably should not exist.

Reviews of the Public Choice Literature

Having shown the inadequacies and limitations of the assumptions of the Tiebout model, I next examine two extensive reviews of the Public Choice literature to ascertain if that literature supports the Tiebout Model. These reviews were conducted by Dowding et al. (1994) and Kay and Marsh (2007).

Dowding et al. derived a number of "testable implications" (768) from the Tiebout model's assumptions and proceeded to examine the empirical literature to learn whether it supported these assumptions. The testable implications fell under five general areas: city size, homogeneity and sorting, capitalization methods, fiscally induced migration and micro-level studies. Dowding et al. then reviewed the literature accordingly.

In each area, the best that the research showed was a possible link to the Tiebout model, but nothing definitive and in some cases the literature could not support the model. Regarding city size, for example, Dowding et al. could not draw any conclusions mainly because of differences in research approaches. Regarding homogeneity and sorting, they said that the literature was consistent with but not corroborative of the Tiebout model. Clearly, they said, sorting occurs, "... but the research shows mixed evidence that local tax and expenditure variables affect the process" (775). These authors could not draw conclusions about capitalization methods, in part because the literature didn't "... directly test whether moving decisions are influenced by local taxes and services" (779). In the area of fiscally induced migration, they found that the literature lends "... considerable support to certain elements of Tiebout's model. However, the use of aggregate level data to test individual decisions is problematic" (784). Additionally, several studies that found possible links here did "... not rule out other alternative models" (784). Finally, the micro-level studies they reviewed produced inconsistent results, although the majority seemed to suggest that factors other than tax-service packages were responsible for household moves.

In the end, Dowding et al. said that while their conclusions from this literature were " ... tentative and disputable ... the Tiebout family of models holds a number of important truths about urban politics" (787). I return to this conclusion after I discuss Kay and Marsh's take on this literature.

Kay and Marsh divided their review of the literature search into three parts, the fiscal mobility literature, evidence from the UK regarding fiscal mobility and the residential mobility literature. They began with a brief history of the fiscal mobility literature and concluded, quoting Dowding et al. that this literature supports " ... at least some of the implications of the Tiebout model" (170). They also agreed with Dowding et al. that methodological problems, mainly the use of aggregate data to infer individual choices, somewhat undermined this conclusion. Thus, the case for fiscal mobility is less than clear cut.

Next, Kay and Marsh examined evidence from the UK regarding fiscal mobility. They began by noting that differences in how local government is structured between the US and the UK make it somewhat difficult to investigate

Tiebout effects in the latter. In any event, they found only two studies in the UK that employed micro-level data to test for Tiebout effects. Both studies found evidence that *some* movers were motivated by the tax-service package.

The issue of *some* then became critical for Kay and Marsh. Here, their question was "how big is big?" (173). In other words, how sizeable must be the fraction movers who move for tax-service reasons to validate the Tiebout model? Clearly the answer is somewhere between none and all, but there is no agreement as to what the appropriate fraction is. One of the two studies Kay and Marsh reviewed (John et al., 1995) argued that if 10 percent of movers were so motivated this would validate the model. This strikes me (as it apparently did Kay and Marsh) as a quite low. Indeed, would a finding that 90 percent of movers are motivated by factors other than the tax-service package not greatly undermine the validity and utility of a model?

Kay and Marsh then reviewed the residential mobility literature and concluded that this literature does not support the Tiebout model. Even if one adopts a "generous interpretation" of that literature, the conclusion that follows is that only "… a relatively modest minority of movers are primarily moving for Tiebout-relevant reasons" (175). These findings led Kay and Marsh to part company with Dowding et al. and to suggest that if the findings of the literature are "tentative and disputable," it is unlikely that there can be "a number of important truths" in them (179). I concur with Kay and Marsh.

Validity and Utility of the Tiebout Model

Where, then, does this leave us regarding the validity and utility of the Tiebout model? I have examined the Tiebout model and have found it wanting because it does not accurately describe objective reality. None of the model's assumptions is empirically accurate. Indeed, the main and fatal weakness of the model is its unrealistic assumptions. In turn, the assumptions cause the model itself to fail because they do not and cannot present an empirically accurate view of how governments and residents of metropolitan areas actually behave.

For example, consumer–voters are not perfectly mobile. They do not have full knowledge of the different tax-service packages in their metropolitan areas. There is a limited number of communities from which a consumer–voter can reasonably choose when selecting a residential location. Where one works may affect the residential locations of consumer–voters. The polycentric metropolitan area produces numerous negative externalities and provides opportunities for achieving economies of scale. There is no "optimal" community size, and governments are hardly economically rational creatures when making decisions regarding taxes and services. Finally, except for the nearly universal effort by US local governments to increase their tax bases, these governments do not act in an economically rational manner regarding the growth or maintenance of their populations.

Even Tiebout himself realized the flaws in the model: "this severe model [the model without easing assumptions] does not make much sense" (421). "Hence

54   *Metropolitan Governance in America*

this model is not even a first approximation of reality" (421). And, finally: "Those who are tempted to compare this model with the competitive private model may be disappointed" (424). At least some other scholars who have followed Tiebout have concurred (for example, Buchanan and Goetz, 1972).

I have also shown that the literature only weakly supports or does not support at all the implications of the model, especially the principal implication that consumer–voters make residential location decisions primarily for reasons predicted by the model.

So, what then, explains the longevity of the Tiebout model? Part of the answer lies in the fact that it is now and has long been a central feature of the Public Choice School. According to Kay and Marsh (2007), the "... Tiebout model is a mainstay of the Public Choice analysis of finance and thus attached to a broader Public Choice research program" (180). As such, it also has a substantial constituency. Moreover, that constituency uses the model in quite normative ways, for example:

> ... to argue that local autonomy, smaller governmental units, less central government intervention, and less inter-jurisdictional redistribution would improve social welfare. These are normatively attractive properties for some policy makers and part of the intellectual foundation of Public Choice theory (Kay and Marsh, 2007: p. 179).

Citing Lakatos (1970), Kay and Marsh also note that, even if proven wrong, scholars are loathe to part with their theories or models, no matter that they are factually inaccurate.

Hill (2008) also noted that:

> Neo-classical economics has a considerable stake in economists' assumptions about preferences being true. If preferences do not accord with economists' assumptions, core axioms of rational choice models, on which economics relies, are violated. Moreover, an important economists' credo is that assumptions need not be realistic or true—just useful; thus, when economists are presented evidence that something they use in their models is not true, they have a ready answer. And in some set of cases, the assumption is indeed useful—because it is true enough. But the assumption is maintained even when it is not useful; economics is loath to cede its elegant parsimony (701–702).

Thus, even though the Tiebout model does not portray reality accurately and has a number of other serious weaknesses, it is supported by a sizeable body of scholars and advocates and is imbedded in the scholarly discourse around metropolitan government and governance. This is so even though the Tiebout model and subsequent Public Choice scholarship fail to address the serious negative externalities affecting metropolitan areas and that have been well known by scholars, practitioners and advocates for at least six decades.

Regardless of the reasons for the perpetuation of this school, what advice do I have for consumers of Public Choice literature about metropolitan government and governance? I approach anything I read from this school with profound skepticism. Public Choice scholarship is driven by strong normative beliefs in certain values (for example, polycentrism, efficiency and localism, among others). This results in a scholarship that follows a fairly consistent pattern in its results and is highly predictable in its findings and recommendations. As such, at least when applied to metropolitan government and governance, Public Choice has become nearer to an ideology than a carefully constructed research paradigm that endeavors to examine matters impartially and objectively. I do not find this literature useful in understanding the serious problems that face metropolitan areas or helpful to local jurisdictions and residents in addressing such problems. Indeed, I find it a hindrance to the achievement of solutions to the overarching problems (read: externalities) that nearly all US metropolitan areas face.

References

Barnett, Jeffrey L. and Phillip M. Vidal. 2013 (July). State and local government finances summary: 2011—Governments Division Briefs. Washington: US Census Bureau. www.census.gov/govs/local. Accessed October 13, 2013.

Bembry, James X. and Donald F. Norris. 2005. An exploratory study of neighborhood choices among moving to opportunity participants in Baltimore, Maryland: The influence of housing search. *Journal of Sociology and Social Welfare*, 32(4): 93–107.

Boadway, Robin and Jean-Francois Tremblay. 2011. Reassessment of the Tiebout model. *Journal of Public Economics*, 96(11–12): 1063–1078.

Boheikm, R. and Mark P. Taylor. 2002. Tied down or room to move: investigating the relationships between housing tenure, employment status and residential mobility in Britain. *Scottish Journal of Political Economy*, 49(4): 369–392.

Buchanan, James M. and Ch.J. Goetz. 1972. Efficiency limits of fiscal mobility: An assessment of the Tiebout model. *Journal of Public Economics*, 1(1): 25–43.

Clark, William A. V. 1992. Residential preferences and residential choices in a multiethnic context. *Demography*, 29(3): 451–466.

Dowding, Keith, Peter John and Stephen Briggs. 1994. Tiebout: A survey of the empirical literature. *Urban Studies*, 31(4/5): 767–797.

Ermisch, John and Pamela Di Salvo. 1996. Surprises and housing tenure decisions in Great Britain. *Journal of Housing Economics*, 5(3): 247–273.

Hill, Claire A. 2008. The rationality of preference construction (and the irrationality of rational choice). *Minnesota Journal of Law, Science and Technology*, 9(2): 698–742.

Howell-Moroney, Michael. 2008. The Tiebout hypothesis 50 years later: Lessons and lingering challenges for metropolitan governance in the 21st century. *Public Administration Review*, 68(1): 97–109.

International City/County Management Association. 2012. Inside the Yearbook. *The Municipal Yearbook: 2013*. Washington, DC: ICMA.

John, Peter, Keith Dowding and Stephen Briggs. 1995. Residential mobility in London: A micro level test of the behavioral assumptions of the Tiebout model. *British Journal of Political Science*, 25(3): 379–397.

Kan, Kamhon. 1999. Expected and unexpected residential mobility. *Journal of Urban Economics*, 45(1): 72–96.

Kay, Adrian and Alex Marsh. 2007. The methodology of the public choice research programme: The case of "Voting With Feet." *New Political Economy*, 12(2): 167–183.

Keating, Michael. 1995. Size, efficiency and democracy: Consolidation, fragmentation and public choice. In David Judge, Gerry Stoke and Hal Wolman (eds), *Theories of Urban Politics*. Thousand Oaks, CA. Sage Publications.

Ladd, Helen F. 1992. Mimicking of local tax burdens among neighboring counties. *Public Finance Review*, 20(4): 450–467.

Lakatos, Imre. 1970. Falisification and the methodology of scientific research Programs. In Imre Lakatos and Alan Musgrave (eds), *Criticism and the Growth of Knowledge*. Cambridge: Cambridge University Press, 91–196.

Lakewood, City of. 2014. Municipal Website. http://www.lakewoodcity.org/about_lakewood/community_profile/the_lakewood_plan.asp. Accessed January 31, 2014.

Lichtenstein, Sarah and Paul Slavic. 2006. The construction of preference: An overview. In Sarah Lichtenstein and Paul Slavic (eds), *The Construction of Preference*. Cambridge: Cambridge University Press, 1–40.

Lowery, David and William E. Lyons. 1989. The impact of jurisdictional boundaries: An individual-level test of the Tiebout model. *Journal of Politics*, 51(1): 73–97.

Neenan, William B. and Marcus E. Ethridge. 1984. Competition and cooperation among localities. In Richard D. Bigham and John P. Blair (eds), *Urban Economic Development*. Beverly Hills, CA: Sage Publications, 175–190.

Norris, Donald F. 2001. Prospects for regional governance under the New Regionalism: Economic imperatives versus political impediments. *Journal of Urban Affairs*, 23(5): 557–571.

Oates, Wallace E. 1969. The effect of property taxes and local public spending on property values: an empirical study of tax capitalization and the Tiebout hypothesis. *Journal of Political Economy*, 77(6): 957–971.

Ostrom, Vincent, Charles M. Tiebout and Robert Warren. 1961. The organization of government in metropolitan areas: A theoretical enquiry. *American Political Science Review*, 55(4): 831–842.

Peterson, Paul. 1981. *City Limits*. Chicago: University of Chicago Press.

Ross, Bernard H. and Myron A. Levine. 1996. *Urban Politics* (5th ed.). New York: Longman.

Rossi, Peter H. 1980. *Why Families Move* (2nd ed.). Beverley Hills, CA: Sage.

Rossi, Peter H. and Anne B. Shlay. 1982. Residential mobility and public policy issues: "Why People Move" revisited. *Journal of Social Issues*, 38(3): 21–34.

Sharp, E. B. 1984. Exit, voice and loyalty in the context of local government problems. *Western Political Quarterly*, 37(1): 67–83.

Shumaker, Sally Ann and Daniel Stokols. 1982. Residential Mobility as a social issue and research topic. *Journal of Social Issues*, 38(3): 1–19.

Simon, Herbert. 1956. Rational choice and the structure of the environment. *Psychological Review*, 63(2): 129–138.

Simon, Herbert. 1957. A behavioral model of rational choice. In Herbert Simon, *Models of Man, Social and Rational: Mathematical Essays on Rational Human Behavior in a Social Setting*. New York: Wiley.

South, Scott J. and Kyle D. Crowder. 1997. Residential mobility between cities and suburbs: Race, suburbanization, and back-to-the-city moves. *Demography*, 34(4): 525–538.

South, Scott J. and Glenn D. Dean. 1993. Race and residential mobility: Individual determinants and structural constraints. *Social Forces*, 70(1): 147–167.

Stein, Robert M. 1987. Tiebout's sorting hypothesis. *Urban Affairs Quarterly*, 23(1): 140–160.

Stephens, G. Ross, and Nelson Wikstrom. 2000. *Metropolitan Government and Governance: Theoretical Perspectives, Empirical Analysis and the Future*. New York: Oxford University Press.

Tiebout, Charles. 1956. A pure theory of local expenditures. *Journal of Political Economy*, 64(5): 416–424.

von Weizsacker, C. Christian. 2005. The welfare economics of adaptive preference. *Preprints of the Max Planck Institute for Research on Collective Goods*. http://www.coll.mpg.de/pdf_dat/2005_11online.pdf. Accessed August 13, 2013.

Williams, Oliver P. 1967. Lifestyle values and political decentralization in metropolitan America. *Southwest Social Science Quarterly*, 48(4): 299–310.

Chapter 4
The New Regionalism

The New Regionalism is the third perspective on metropolitan government and governance that I examine. The New Regionalism came into being in the late 1980s and early 1990s and is seen by some scholars (myself included) as an expansion of and modification to the works of the Metropolitan Reformers. In large part, the New Regionalism arose because of the failure of the old regionalism (aka, the Metro Reform movement) to achieve any significant foothold in practice in American metropolitan areas (see also Sancton, 2001; Kantor, 2006). As I noted in the Chapter 2, only a scant few regions around the country have adopted meaningful structural reform in the past 60 plus years, and no region boasts structural reforms that today are metro-wide.[1]

The New Regionalism expands the work of the Metropolitan Reformers by arguing that global economic competitiveness is the principal rationale for metropolitan governance. More specifically, the New Regionalism asserts that, because regions in the US need to be economically competitive with regions around the world, American local governments should and will cooperate in ways that will produce governance across their metropolitan areas.

The New Regionalism modifies the solutions proposed by the Metropolitan Reformers by shifting away from structural reform to intergovernmental cooperation. This is almost undoubtedly because structural reform has almost completely failed to be adopted in US metropolitan areas, and there is little likelihood that structural reform will be adopted by even a small fraction of regions anytime in the foreseeable future. Thus, the New Regionalism places hope for the development of metropolitan governance on what I will show is the very slim reed of voluntary cooperation among the local governments. Still, the main focus of the New Regionalism, like that of the Metro Reform movement, is to address the negative externalities that have occurred as the result of metropolitan fragmentation and the relatively uncontrolled growth and development in the post-Second World War American metropolitan areas.

In the following pages, I describe the New Regionalism as it is presented in the New Regionalist literature. Second, I discuss the essential differences and similarities between the New Regionalism and the Metropolitan Reformers. Third, I address the New Regionalism's assertion that global economic competition among regions exists, and that this competition will impel local governments to cooperate in

---

1   It is conceivable that, when some structural reforms were initially adopted, they encompassed entire metropolitan areas. However, as metro areas grew, the boundaries of these structures, for the most part, did not grow..

order to address the negative externalities that have been produced by metropolitan fragmentation and growth. Fourth, I examine the New Regionalist claim of suburban dependency—that is, that suburbs are dependent for their economic well-being on the health of their central cities. Fifth, I review international research on metropolitan governance and cooperation as it might be relevant to our understanding of the New Regionalism. Finally, I conclude by noting that the New Regionalism is as unlikely as the Metro Reform movement before it (for both similar and different reasons) to produce metropolitan governance anywhere in the US.

What is the New Regionalism?

In a symposium in *State and Local Government Review* in 2000, two of the foremost advocates of the New Regionalism, H. V. Savitch and Ronald Vogel argued that the New Regionalism is "both a policy agenda and a set of public interventions" (158). The need for the New Regionalism, they further argued, arose out of the sprawling and fragmented local government landscape of postwar America. Uncontrolled growth and governmental fragmentation, they claimed, have produced serious negative externalities affecting entire metro areas and especially their central cities and near-in suburbs. According to Savitch and Vogel, these externalities include "ever widening social disparities between central cities and suburbs, as well as between older and newer suburbs" (160). Other negative externalities found in the New Regionalist literature include: fiscal disparities between cities and suburbs, class and racial segregation, concentrated poverty, spatial mismatch, lack of affordable housing, environmental degradation, infrastructure needs and costs, and the loss of farmland and wetlands (see, for example, Savitch and Vogel, 2000; Brenner, 2002; Wheeler, 2002). As one can see, this list of negative externalities is strikingly similar to any list that could be found in the writings of the Metro Reformers.

According to Savitch and Vogel (2000), New Regionalists, among other things, "seek to contain sprawl by invoking growth boundaries and land preservation trusts; they intend to reduce economic disparities through tax sharing ... they seek to combine city and suburban resources to better compete in a global economy" (161). In 2007, Harrigan and Vogel wrote that the New Regionalism agenda included addressing fiscal disparities, racial and class segregation, sprawl, and "reurbanizing the city" (300). These objectives would be achieved principally through voluntary cooperation, which, in their view, was the more likely route to metro governance than structural reform.

Global economic competition and suburban dependency are two important additional elements of the New Regionalism. Indeed, this addition to the metropolitan governance conversation has fundamentally altered the rationale for such governance (for example, Swanstrom, 1996 and 2001).

First, the New Regionalism claims that because regions face global competition for economic survival, suburbs should and, indeed, will engage in cooperative efforts with other suburbs and their central cities to ensure that the entire region prospers economically (Savitch and Vogel, 2001). In the view of the New Regionalism, suburbs will do this not out of altruism or to achieve the greater good for the entire metropolitan area, but rather because they must to prosper economically. Simply put, economic necessity will overcome the political barriers to metropolitan governance in US regions.

Second, the New Regionalism argues that the very economic health of suburbs is inexorably tied to the health of their central cities (for example Savitch et al., 1993). This has come to be known as the suburban dependency hypothesis. This, therefore, is a second important reason for suburbs to cooperate with their central cities. Economic necessity again trumps politics.

The New Regionalism literature distinguishes between *governance* and *government*. Indeed, the distinction between government and governance is critical to understanding the New Regionalism. New Regionalists eschew *government*, those pesky formal structures that seem to get in the way of governance. In its place, the New Regionalists argue that intergovernmental cooperation, especially voluntary cooperation between suburbs and central cities, will produce something called *governance*. Governance through voluntary cooperation, in turn, will directly affect change in the metropolitan area and will enable the New Regionalism to achieve the goals of addressing the negative externalities of sprawl and fragmentation and of regional economic competitiveness.

The term governance is widely employed throughout the New Regionalism literature. Yet, it is rarely if ever concretely described or defined. It is possible to infer from this literature, however, that governance involves voluntary cooperation among public sector organizations (for example, local governments). Cooperation may also include non-governmental organizations (both for profit and not for profit). A clear emphasis in this literature is on a variety of actors across entire metropolitan areas coming together to address these regions' most difficult problems. Doing so, in turn, will enable regions to become competitive in the global economy. One can also infer from this literature that to the New Regionalists, cooperation is, indeed, the only route available for regions to achieve a state of global economic competitiveness.

Unfortunately, this literature rarely if ever specifies in concrete ways how cooperation produces governance and how governance, in turn, produces regional competitiveness in the global economy. One possible exception could be if suburbs take action to strengthen declining central cities (something claimed by the New Regionalism but hardly ever seen in practice). According to the New Regionalism, this would somehow strengthen entire regions and make them globally competitive. Again, however, New Regionalists assert much here, but concretely describe little.

In the end, perhaps the best understanding of the New Regionalism from its own writings is that something called governance (aka, voluntary intergovernmental and intersectoral cooperation) will occur in American metropolitan areas because of the imperatives of global economic competition and suburban dependency.

Metropolitan governance will then: 1) address the negative externalities of fragmentation and sprawl (of which aiding the poor central cities is one); and 2) will make regions competitive in the global economy. Structural reform is neither desirable nor needed.

It is, at the very least, interesting that among the articles published in this Symposium, all but one of the metropolitan reforms presented as examples of the New Regionalism were, in fact, structural reforms when the New Regionalism explicitly rejects structural reform in favor of voluntary cooperation (Savitch and Vogel, 2000). The structural reforms reviewed were: city–county consolidation (Indianapolis and Jacksonville); annexation and functional consolidation (Charlotte); failed consolidation efforts up to 2000 (Louisville); consolidation (in small Georgia cities and counties). The sole exception came from a Public Choice scholar.

Metropolitan Reformers and the New Regionalism

The New Regionalism is similar in one very important way to the Metropolitan Reform School. The Metropolitan Reformers and New Regionalists are quite vexed by the negative externalities that, they have argued, flow from fragmentation and sprawl. And, the central purpose of their writings of both schools is to provide mechanisms to address those externalities.

The New Regionalists and the Metro Reformers, however, part company when it comes to how to address these externalities. As I showed in Chapter 2, the Metro Reformers called mainly for structural reforms and governmental intervention. The New Regionalists call for voluntary cooperation. "Ultimately New Regionalism requires that communities look outward to the larger metropolis and consider their collective future" (Savitch and Vogel, 2000, p. 161). What is good for the overall region is good for each of its collective parts, or so the argument goes.

There are three additional important differences between the New Regionalism and the Metropolitan Reformers. The first of these is the New Regionalism's emphasis on global economic competitiveness. The second is its argument that the health of suburbs is dependent on the health of the central city. The third is the New Regionalist's assertion that cooperation among local governments in metropolitan areas will produce metropolitan governance which, in turn, will address the negative externalities of fragmentation and sprawl, and which will make regions economically competitive. I address each of these in the following sections.

Do Regions Compete?

As I have previously noted, the New Regionalists have fundamentally changed the rationale for regional reform. It is no longer based on equity, efficiency or good will, but rather on the assertion that regions must become and remain competitive in the global economy. According to Savitch and Vogel, cooperation among local governments is necessary in order to "combine city and suburban resources to better compete in a global economy" (161). In Swanstrom's words (2001), "a central thread in new regionalist literature is that regional reforms will improve the economic competitiveness of regions in the global economy" (480). Swanstrom also noted that "the argument of much of the [New Regionalism] literature is that spatial inequalities should be opposed not just because they are unfair but also because they will harm regional economic competitiveness" (482).

New Regionalists make two distinct assertions here. First, regions compete, and, second, the imperative of global economic competition will impel local governments (and other actors) in regions to cooperate because that cooperation will ensure that their regions will be economically competitive. Both assertions raise empirical questions. Does global economic competition exist? Does it affect regions as the New Regionalists say? That is, do regions really compete with one another in the global economy? Do local governments actually cooperate with one another, and if they do, is it to ensure the economic health of the overall region because of global economic competition? In the following sections I address both assertions.

There can be no question that the economy is truly global today. Indeed, it has been for a very long time. But, it is a very long step from this blinding flash of the obvious to the assertion that regions around the world compete with one another. Is it true, for example, that metropolitan areas in the US compete with regions in Europe, Asia and elsewhere (and vice versa) for economic growth? Certainly firms (that are located in cities, suburbs and regions) compete internationally. But, do regions, per se, compete?

For a region to compete, certain conditions would have to be met. The most important of these is that a large fraction of important public, private and non-profit actors in a region would have to come together and agree upon a set of goals and objectives for the region to pursue. One would imagine that these goals and objectives would principally be economic in nature to meet the New Regionalists' argument that regions must be competitive in the global economy.

Here is how I would envision regional decision-making occurring, were it to follow the model set forth by the New Regionalists:

> As a region, we intend to be the very best worldwide in widget making (or whatever). All decisions that we make as a region will be linked directly to achieving this objective. We will make no decisions of consequence that are not consistent with this objective. We will allocate the region's budgetary and other scarce resources accordingly. And we will do all of this voluntarily.[2]

What I cannot imagine, however, is that actors in any region in the US (or perhaps elsewhere in the free world) would be willing or able to act in such a manner,

---

2 Who the authoritative decision-makers are remains a mystery.

whether to achieve economic or other objectives. There are at least four reasons why actors in regions cannot and would not engage in such decision-making. First, too many actors are involved. Even small regions contain large numbers of actors, and there are legions more actors in large regions. The greater the number of actors, the lower is the likelihood that they can agree on anything (for example, Pressman and Wildavsky, 1984). This would be especially true if an agreement would require individual actors (especially local governments) to allocate their resources to the benefit of other actors (read: suburbs to central cities or, indeed, to other suburbs).

Second, the actors in regions represent too many differing points of view, desires, values, needs, and so on. Even in smaller regions, with their relatively smaller numbers of actors, differences among actors cancel out the ability to agree, except in the most general sense, on important things like whether and how to address negative externalities, whether and how to assist declining central cities, goals for economic development and many others. Third, even if a substantial number of actors in a region could join together and come to agreement on economic development goals and objectives, voluntary cooperation has no teeth (Norris, 2001a). It is the weakest weapon in the arsenal of intergovernmental affairs (for example, Downs, 1992 and 1994; Downs and Puentes, 2005; Walker, 1987). Any actor or actors can walk away from voluntary agreements, and there is no way to compel compliance with voluntary cooperation. The lowest common denominator prevails (Norris 2001a).

Fourth, the entire idea of cooperation around difficult issues completely ignores politics. In US metropolitan areas, the chief political characteristic that limits and often prevents cooperation (to say nothing of agreements that are legally binding), especially on tough issues like addressing the negative externalities of fragmentation and sprawl and assisting declining central cities, is local government autonomy (Norris 2001a and 2001b; Danielson 1976). Local governments are loath to give up even a tiny fraction of their autonomy.[3] Local governments' interests and motivations largely begin and end with their boundaries and their residents. For this reason, and also because local residents will penalize local elected officials in future elections for behaving otherwise, local governments look to the good of their territories and their citizens, not the good of their region. Lastly, suburban officials have little or no incentives to take actions that will, for example, help redistribute wealth to the advantage of their central cities because the suburbs' constituents do not want their money spent on bailing out those cities.

---

3   I realize that the Dillon rule says that local governments are not autonomous. To a large extent, however, state governments tend to leave locals alone on many of the issues arising out of the negative externalities about which both the Metro Reformers and New Regionalists are concerned. Additionally, and to a large extent, local governments act like they are autonomous over these and many other issues, and state governments tend to act similarly.

Certainly, firms within regions compete, and today nearly all firms of any consequence compete globally. One of the great weaknesses, however, of the New Regionalism's competitiveness imperative is that it equates regions with firms (Lovering, 1999). " ... [R]egions are not commensurate with firms. To speak of competitiveness at the level of the firm is to point out that it [a firm] must survive against rivals producing competing products or services" (389). But, since the economic well-being of a region cannot be measured by a single value, conceptualizing regions in the same manner as firms is not helpful and "befuddles rather than illuminates this question" (389).[4]

The largest firms, wherever headquartered, are international in nearly every way. But, here is the important part—firms compete; they do not just cooperate with one another. Whether auto manufacturers, pharmaceutical companies, grocery chains or mom and pop stores, they compete for customers, market share, profits and more. The interests and motivations of firms are far different from those of local governments. Firms are focused on the bottom line (profit) and on returning value to their shareholders where local governments are focused on such things as delivering services, maintaining order and upholding the norms of democracy. These are not economic values.

Furthermore, firms' views of what is best for their regions differ, even among firms in the same market. For example, in 2013, the Maryland General Assembly, the state legislature in my home state, voted to increase the tax on gasoline in order to better fund transportation improvements in the state. These improvements mainly benefited the large urban areas of the state. Firms that depended more heavily on the state's highway infrastructure were more likely to support this tax than firms that did not. Firms in this urban area were more likely than firms in rural areas of the state to support this tax.

In another example, a rival, out-of-state grocery chain recently sought to have a parcel of property in my community of Columbia, Maryland, rezoned in order to build a high-end store. A group of local residents coalesced to oppose the rezoning on the basis that it would increase traffic congestion unacceptably. One of the supporters of this coalition was a well-known statewide grocery chain that did not welcome competition from the out-of-state firm that, coincidentally, was a non-union shop when the in-state firm was unionized

Because firms compete and because they view public policy through the lens of what benefits the firm (versus the region, the state or the nation), it is hard to imagine that firms would come together and agree on all but the most general of goals for their regions. Here, too, it is hard to imagine that firms, any more than local governments, would agree to share their resources with other firms (or governments) in the region or that they would agree to anything that would be binding, especially anything that would erode their independence and profitabilty.

---

4 Lovering was writing about regions as defined by the Labour Party in the UK in the 1990s. Nevertheless, his argument about regions not being the same as firms is relevant here.

The New Regionalists also assert that local governments must and will cooperate to achieve metropolitan governance and address the negative externalities resulting from sprawl and fragmentation, all to achieve a state of global economic competitiveness. The question, however, is whether local governments actually behave this way. That is, do they really cooperate with one another, and, if they do, is it in order to make their regions economically competitive? Here again, we need to look at the evidence.

There is no doubt from the vast urban literature in the United States that local governments cooperate voluntarily with one another (among others, see: Dye et al., 1963; Feiock, 2007; Hawkins, 2010; Olberding, 2002; Thompson, 1997). It is also clear that they cooperate most often around systems maintenance versus lifestyle issues (Williams, 1967; see also Chapter 5). The latter finding is in direct contrast to the argument of the New Regionalists who claim that cooperation is sufficient to address the really tough issues that affect regions—the negative externalities of fragmentation and sprawl. If local governments do not cooperate voluntarily around those issues—and the preponderance of evidence shows that they do not –they can hardly address them. The evidence in Chapter 5 also shows that, for the most part, even the leaders of regional organizations do not think much of the ability of cooperation to address these issues.

What is absent from the literature is any evidence that local governments are motivated to cooperate by the real or perceived need to ensure that their regions are economically competitive. For the most part they cooperate in order to address service-related issues, not to address externalities and especially not to address fiscal and other inequities arising from those externalities. Nor do they cooperate when cooperation would infringe on their autonomy or negatively affect their budgets, and certainly not if cooperation involves redistribution of their resources to other local governments.

Nor do cities and suburbs necessarily cooperate when cooperation appears to be in their self-interests. In 1997, Myron Orfield showed that, because of shared interests, central city–suburban coalitions in the Minneapolis-St. Paul region could and did work cooperatively together to lobby their state legislature to get policies and support from the Minnesota state government. From this experience, he reasoned this sort of cooperation between central cities and their near-in suburbs might work in other states. On its face, this seems to make good sense because, in many regions, near-in suburbs look much like their central cities and face many of the same problems (for example, Vicino, 2008; Hanlon and Vicino, 2007).

Weir et al. (2005) sought to verify Orfield's claim and conducted a study of central city lobbying of state legislatures in Illinois, Michigan, Ohio and New York. They found just the opposite—central cities and near-in suburbs do not cooperate in this manner. Instead, even though on an objective basis, poor central cities and older suburbs have similar interests in certain types of state legislation, big city mayors did not pursue coalitions with suburbs and, when they did, suburbs declined to participate, fearing domination by the big cities' interests.

For all of these reasons, it is very unlikely that local governments or other actors will or even can actually come together and agree on goals and objectives for their regions, the New Regionalists' regional competitiveness argument to the contrary notwithstanding. Indeed, I know of no region in the US, or elsewhere for that matter, where anything remotely similar to this has occurred, especially on a voluntary basis.

Suburban Dependency

As noted previously, the New Regionalists argue that local governments in metropolitan areas will cooperate with one another to enhance the well-being of the region in order to keep it competitive in the global economy. The New Regionalists take this argument one step further and claim that economic health of the suburbs depends on the economic health of the central city and that this will also compel suburbs to cooperate with one another and the central city to ensure the economic health of the latter and, along with it, the region (Savitch et al., 1993). This is known as suburban dependency hypothesis. Considerable scholarly research has been conducted around this hypothesis, some of which indicates not only a link here but causality, suggesting that the health of the suburbs is indeed dependent on the health of the city (Blair and Zhang, 1994; Ledebur and Barnes, 1992 and 1993; Savitch et al., 1993; Voith, 1992). However, yet other studies question the link, the causality or both (for example, Hill et al., 1995; Post and Stein, 2000). In the following paragraphs, I briefly discuss research on both sides of the suburban dependency hypothesis.

The first two works that I examine in this vein were written by Ledebur and Barnes and published as monographs by the National League of Cities in 1992 and 1993. Each is quite short, 18 pages and 13 pages, plus appendices, respectively. Each is also clearly an advocacy piece. And, considering the frequency with which they have been cited in the debate around suburban dependency, each has had an outsized impact. In the first work, *Metropolitan Disparities and Economic Growth*, Ledebur and Barnes (1992) used employment and unemployment rates in metro areas to show that "Economic disparities between central cities and suburbs increased sharply in the 1980s retard regional economic growth" (1). No one would argue that during the 1980s, urban–suburban economic well-being diverged considerably. However, it is one thing to show disparity and quite another to make the claims found in this paper.

The first claim is that the central city–suburban economic disparity retards regional economic growth. The second is that the nation's economic growth is dependent on growth in regions. The third is that, therefore, national economic policies are needed to address the growing disparities between cities and their suburbs. Ledebur and Barnes, next, claimed that central cities and suburbs are economically interdependent (a claim few would dispute), but they then took the claim two steps further. Because central cities and suburbs are economically interdependent, they have a common interest in regional economic growth, and, therefore, central cities and their suburbs should and will work together for the common economic good within their regions. None of these claims can be sustained by reference only to employment and unemployment rates. But, never mind, the point of the monograph was to call for national policies to aid the National League of Cities' members, especially declining central cities. For that purpose, not a lot of evidence was evidently needed.

In their second piece, *All in it Together*, Ledebur and Barnes (1993) examined 25 metro areas with the most rapidly growing suburbs (note the sample bias here) to once again show disparities between central cities and suburbs. Once again, they claimed that central cities and their suburbs are economically interdependent, and once again the notion of interdependence is hardly new or controversial. Ledebur and Barnes went beyond interdependence, however, and asked rhetorically whether suburbs can succeed, survive or prosper if their central cities do not, suggesting that the well-being of the suburbs is somehow dependent on that of central cities. Again Ledebur and Barnes used only descriptive statistics—median household income and employment and unemployment rates in this case—to make their argument. And once again, it is hard for serious urban scholars to find sufficient support from such data for the claims made in the work.

In a work published by the Federal Reserve Bank of Philadelphia in 1992, Voith examined growth in the central cities and suburbs of 28 metro areas in the northeastern and North Central US over a 30-year period. His interest was to understand the relationship between central city and suburban economies, particularly whether these were substitutes or complements. He found a positive correlation between city and suburban population, income and employment growth for these metropolitan areas. This led Voith to conclude that central "... cities and suburbs are compliments" (31). He went on to argue: "From a policy perspective, the evidence of complementarity suggests that both city and suburb could improve their welfare through actions to arrest urban decline" (31).

Unfortunately, the statistical technique that Voith used was bivariate correlation analysis and as Voith, himself, understood "Simple correlations between city and suburban growth must be interpreted with care" (25). This is because simple correlations tell us nothing about causation or about the direction of correlation. Hence, Voith's work is at best suggestive; certainly not definitive. And, his policy advice to address urban decline, while probably not bad advice, cannot be said to follow from his findings.

In 1993, Savitch et al. used a variety of measures to claim that central cities and suburbs are interdependent. They argued that because central cities and suburbs are interdependent, both will do better economically if they work together cooperatively. They wrote: "... cities and suburbs do best when they interact and make use of respective and complementary strengths. We refer to the ability of cities to encompass and harness the assets of the larger region as inclusion.

Inclusion can take different forms, ranging from outright annexation, to interlocal agreements to informal partnerships" (349).[5]

Clearly, their intent was to show that if the health of the suburbs is dependent on the health of the central city, the suburbs then *should* engage with their central cities to help them. Once again, the prescriptive aims of the New Regionalism are evident. However, as various scholars have shown, the obvious problem with this work is that bivariate correlation analysis, the method Savitch et al. used, cannot prove causation (for example, Hill et al., 1995; Swanstrom, 1996 and 2001). So we are left, at best, with an asserted but not demonstrated relationship. What is more, the evidence from various studies, as well as simple observation, seems to suggest that some suburbs may well be dependent on their central cities; others may be the engines of economic development in their regions; and others yet, "Edge Cities," may be independent (Garreau, 1991).

Hill et al. (1995), examined works that make the suburban dependency claim and criticized them for at least two reasons. First, these works employ bivariate correlation analysis "... that does not test causality and does not control for likely influences on aggregate economic performance" (150). Moreover, while Hill et al. agreed with the common sense observation that central cities and suburbs are interdependent, they also noted that there can be regions with poor, even extremely poor central cities and healthy suburbs.

This is consistent with what Bradbury et al. found in 1982—at least five categories of metropolitan areas. 1) Growing cities in growing metro areas; 2) stagnant cities and growing metro areas; 3) severely declining cities in growing metro areas; 4) stagnant cities in declining metro areas; and 5) severely declining cities in declining metro areas. This variety of potential interdependencies between central cities and suburbs is greater and more nuanced than the New Regionalists claim. Furthermore, the categories that Bradbury et al. identified show that there can be growth in cities and their suburbs, decline in both and mixed results.

Hill et al. 1995, developed an alternative to the suburban dependency hypothesis and call it the "tight labor market hypothesis" (151). This hypothesis argues that economic growth is a regional phenomenon and that the well-being of central cities and suburbs "... depends partly on the proportion of the metropolitan area's population that resides in the central city ..." (153). In metropolitan areas like Phoenix, AZ, for example, where the central city is "elastic" and encompasses a large fraction of the regional population, income and other disparities between central city and suburbs are lessened.

I would go further and argue that in some metropolitan areas, Baltimore, MD being one, it is the suburbs that are driving regional economic growth (see also Post and Stein, 2000). At some point in the decade of the 1960s, Baltimore's suburbs

---

5   This appears to be a disingenuous use of the term inclusion because each of the examples, and especially annexation, in reality, means central cities taking from suburbs, especially so when these authors said that inclusion means for cities to "harness the assets of the larger region."

exceeded the city in population, and, in the decade of the 1970s, the suburbs exceeded the city in employment. In 1950, Baltimore's total property valuation was nearly triple that of its suburbs. By the early 1960s, the total property valuation of the suburbs exceeded that of the city. I suspect that this pattern is true for many other Frostbelt cities that have been in decline for 60 years or more. Baltimore and its counterparts, thus, represent cases where the central city needs the regional growth created by the suburbs, and it is the city's health that is dependent on the performance of the suburbs, not vice versa.

Another criticism of the studies purporting to demonstrate suburban dependency is that they omit state-level variables that undoubtedly influence regional performance. Hill et al. (1995) made this point and also cited an article by Blair and Zhang (1994) that first noted the importance of state economic development. According to Blair and Zhang, "The addition of appropriate state-level economic development indicators [to their regression model] suggests that correlations between city and suburban economic development may be attributable to state development, rather than to central-city and suburban interdependence" (375).

Post and Stein (2000) conducted yet another study that examined works claiming suburban dependency. Unlike Blair and Zhang, however, they found "... a positive and significant relationship between the economies of central cities and their suburbs that is independent of the state economy" (56). However, they concluded that even though there was a relationship between the economic health of cities and their suburbs, their model could not determine the direction of causation, and, "... in some cases, it is possible that the suburbs are the regional economic engines" (57).

The conclusion that I draw from these studies is that the suburban dependency hypotheses lacks adequate supporting evidence and, therefore, cannot be sustained. Moreover, there are other ways to understand the "ties that bind" (or don't bind) between central cities and their suburbs (for example, the tight labor market hypotheses, state economic variables, the suburban growth engine, and so on).

But even if the suburban dependency hypothesis were true, would suburbs actually behave as the New Regionalists claim they will? As Swanstrom (2001) observed: "It is important to note that even if new regionalist policies could be proven to enhance economic growth, this does not necessarily mean that citizens should support them" (498). I would add that even if citizens *should* support such policies in someone's ideal world, there is little or no evidence to suggest that they actually do so or in the future would do so in the real world. This is because no matter the evidence, the great majority of suburban residents do not believe that their well-being is dependent on that of the central city. For this reason, too, they are not likely to want to or permit their local governments to use their scarce resources or to give up any of their autonomy to bail out the declining central city.

Findings from International Research

Next I examine research from Europe that bears directly on the New Regionalism, including studies of the New Regionalism in Scotland and Holland and of metropolitan governance in England and Poland. I also briefly summarize the conclusions of a recent book (Kantor et al., 2012), co-authored by one of the leading figures in the New Regionalism, about the governability of large city regions.

In two separate papers, Kantor examined the New Regionalism in the Glasgow, Scotland region (2000), and in the Randstad area of Holland, a region that that includes Amsterdam, Rotterdam, The Hague and Utrecht (2006). I begin with Glasgow.

The case of Glasgow (2000) is especially interesting because it focuses on the New Regionalist's claims of suburban dependency and of economic necessity. That is, because suburbs are dependent on central cities for their economic well-being, out of economic necessity they will cooperate with one another and will aid their central cities in order to survive in the global economy. Kantor's study is also interesting because Glasgow appears to have possessed conditions that would facilitate cooperation as it lacked "… the conflicts over race, ethnicity, or partisanship that have often undermined the activities of regional governments elsewhere" (798). Moreover, for the 25 years prior to Kantor's study, economic development in the Glasgow region was "dominated by a powerful regional development institution …," the Scottish Enterprise (SE), originally named the Scottish Development Agency (798).

Yet during this period, Glasgow's population declined by about one-third, leaving it much like many older American central cities, increasingly poor and ringed by well-off suburbs. According to Kantor, this was quite ironic because Glasgow's downward spiral occurred despite what he described as " … massive planning and governmental intervention for decades" (801). Although the planning and intervention initially worked in Glasgow's favor, ultimately the focus of development changed to favor the suburbs.

Why did this happen? The simple answer is political competition and, not unlike in the US, the suburbs were the winners. After discounting alternative explanations, Kantor wrote:

> Specifically, the Scottish experience suggests that governmental intervention … does not necessarily facilitate assistance to needy central cities. The flaw in the reform model is that it conflates abstract notions of regional economic interdependence with prescriptions to aid cities. It neglects the reality that regional interests are a matter of political choice not economic determinism (816).

In his study of the Randstad (2006), Kantor noted that this area of Holland displays "conditions that reform theorists general have considered ideal for the growth of political cooperation" (806). They included: 1) the new economy, 2) limited

72 *Metropolitan Governance in America*

social polarization and 3) centralized government that could make regionalism easier to accomplish. Actual results on the ground, however, tended quite in the opposite direction.

This is because rather than integrating the region, the new economy divided it, with various public and private interests moving in the direction of their own interests and few showing any interest in integration or cooperation. Instead of limited social polarization leading to cooperation, what Kantor calls "bottom up" and "top down fragmentation" and central city–suburban animosity led to a decided lack of cooperation in the region. And, finally, Holland's centralized system of governance impeded local cooperation because "… central government works to organize urban policies around functional bureaucratic domains, often making regional cooperation irrelevant to what the ministries actually do" (820). Once again, political considerations militated against regional cooperation.

Next, I review my study of regional governance and cooperation in England (Norris, 2001a). In this study, I examined the extent to which metropolitan governance occurred in two large conurbations (metro areas) in England—Greater Manchester and the West Midlands (Birmingham and its region). I undertook this study ten years after the British Parliament abolished the metropolitan governments for these and five other conurbations in the country. I was especially interested to learn whether metropolitan governance occurred in the Manchester and Birmingham regions in the absence of formal governmental structures. The short answer is no; and the short reason why is politics.

Here is the longer, though still abbreviated, story. In the course of the study, I interviewed widely among the elected leaders and appointed chief executives in the municipalities of both regions. I also interviewed representatives of the associations of municipalities and representatives of the regional offices of central government in both regions.

The results of these interviews plus a careful reading of the scholarly literature in Britain about the former metropolitan governments and their abolition led to the inescapable conclusion that local politics, mainly around the autonomy or perceived autonomy of local governments in these conurbations, had prevented the development of regional governance in the regions in the years since the metropolitan governments had been abolished.

As one informant, an elected leader, said:

> Governance is independently held by each of the [municipalities]. As a leader, I would not accept any non-legislated [by central government] interference in the day-to-day affairs of the [municipality] … As a leader, you are responsible to your own [municipality] and to your colleagues (Norris, 2001a, p. 541).

All of the officials I interviewed responded in similar terms. Thus, the autonomy of their local governments was central to these officials' views about metropolitan governance. Having lost autonomy (and power) previously, they were of no mind to lose it again. The interviews also revealed continued animosity toward the metro governments long after their abolition as well as the total lack of support among local officials to reestablish those governments or to establish any form of areawide government like them in scope of function.

I also inquired about intergovernmental cooperation in these regions. Two findings stand out. First, in abolishing the metropolitan governments, Parliament distributed many of those governments' prior functions to regional agencies. Parliament allocated some of these functions to the local governments in the regions (for example, trading standards, funding for the arts, planning for public transportation funding, and so on). It placed other functions into structures that included strong central government participation (for example, police, fire, public transportation, airports, and so on). For the most part, the latter were single function entities, akin to many special districts in the US. This legislative disposition created governmental structures and rules that either precluded or left little room for voluntary intergovernmental cooperation across a range of functions in these regions.

Nevertheless, both regions had structures for informal cooperation, namely local government associations that are somewhat similar to regional councils or Councils of Government (or COGs) in the US. Yet, these organizations rarely dealt with controversial issues, and local autonomy influenced nearly all the actions that they took (or failed to take). Their behavior and decisions suffered for the least common denominator effect. According to one official, "Any single MDC [municipality] could and would get its way, regardless of the positions of the others. The actions of joint committees [regional bodies], at least on important matters, had to be unanimous, and achieving unanimity on matters that were controversial or that divided the MDCs was difficult" (Norris, 2001a: p. 531).

I now report on research on metropolitan cooperation and governance in Poland—a book chapter by Marta Lackowska (2007) and a paper that Lackowska and I co-authored (2014). In her book chapter, Lackowska cited literature that argued that voluntary cooperation among local governments in regions can be "... good solution to the metropolitan management problem" (135). She then examined the situation in two Polish metro areas dominated by their central cities, Warsaw and Wroclaw. In the Warsaw region, Lackowska found that cooperation was nearly non-existent. Instead; "Conflicts between neighboring municipalities and the core city are a permanent element of the metropolitan scene" (144). In Wroclaw, by contract, she found a long history of cooperation among the region's jurisdictions as well as engagement across a number of functions and services. However, cooperation in the Wroclaw region was mobilized primarily by the core city, with the suburbs acting passively. As a result, Lackowska wondered whether cooperation of this nature could be successful.

In our co-authored work, Lackowska and I reported findings from a comparative study of the Poland and the US, two nations with widely differing histories, cultures and political–institutional arrangements, to address metropolitan governance in both countries. After brief discussions of metropolitan areas in both national nations, we focused on similarities and differences between those nations insofar as they are relevant to the subject of metropolitan governance. We also investigated factors that either supported or impeded the development of metropolitan governance in regions in Poland and the US. We found that metropolitan governance cannot be said to exist in either nation.

Moreover, we found that, despite numerous contextual differences, the factors responsible for failure of metropolitan governance to develop were highly similar in both nations. These common factors included: 1) the strength of the local level, particularly the unwillingness of local governments to surrender their autonomy; 2) lack of citizen support, which, of course, is related to the previous factor; and 3) the absence of pressure for metropolitan reform from any sector, public or private.

Taken together, these three factors mean that metropolitan reform in both Poland and the US remains very low on the political agenda, if it is on it at all. This is another way of saying that, intentionally or not, the status quo is much more likely to be preserved than threatened. Because of the strength of these factors, we concluded that the current pattern of metropolitan affairs in both countries is likely to persist into the foreseeable future if not a lot longer.

The lesson from these studies of the New Regionalism and metropolitan governance in Scotland, Holland, England and Poland is that in the absence of overarching structures of metropolitan governance, such governance is not likely to arise organically. Local politics will prevent it. Moreover, even when structures exist to address certain areawide functions, such as regional economic development in Scotland, the results will not always be consistent with the claims made by the New Regionalists. In that case, local development politics redirected aid away from Glasgow, a declining central city, to its wealthier surburban neighbors.

The final work I examine offers somewhat of a delicious irony to scholars who are critical of the premises and claims of the New Regionalism. Entitled *Struggling Giants: City-Region Governance in London, New York, Paris and Tokyo*, this is an examination of these four large, international cities, written by Kantor et al. (2012). The irony here is found in the co-authorship of H.V. Savitch, one of the foremost New Regionalist scholars, and the conclusions about governance that the authors, including Savitch, draw from this study.

The principal question that this very ambitious work asks is whether global city-regions (GCRs)—that is, large, international cities and the suburban areas that surround them—are governable. After painstakingly examining these GCRs, the authors conclude that, although "Judging governability is difficult ..." (p. 269), it is possible to do so through the lens of a tripartite frame work that includes *integrated governance* (the strictest definition of governance), *polycentric competition* (the antithesis of integrated governance) and *pragmatic adjustment* (a middle ground between the two extremes of governance).

By the strictest definition, governance was not to be found in any of these regions, and the authors were not sanguine that it would occur there in the future. In addition, all of the regions studied exhibited a greater or lesser degree of fragmentation, polycentrism and competition. However, at the same time, the local governments in each of these regions engaged in pragmatic adjustment over a range of issues and services—that is, they cooperated both formally and informally with one another. But, the authors also concluded that the local governments in these regions were not able to engage in sufficient pragmatic adjustment to address the really tough areawide problems confronting them. Finally, the authors presented no evidence that this situation is likely to change. Hence, the conclusion that I draw from this work is that governance of nearly any sort (except among individual local governments, areawide and functional authorities and the like)—certainly not metropolitan governance—does not occur in these regions, and there is no reason to believe that it will in foreseeable future.

Conclusion

Regardless of the promises of the New Regionalism, it is nearly impossible to find examples of regions in the US or elsewhere in the world in which local governments have voluntarily surrendered their autonomy or voluntarily opened their purse strings in order to better serve the entire metropolitan area and its central city. Notwithstanding the claims of the New Regionalism, nowhere have local governments succumbed to the cry of regional economic competitiveness to work with one another on a voluntary basis to address the really tough, controversial and divisive issues faced by metropolitan areas. This is because the premises and claims of the New Regionalism are highly questionable and most of them fail the test of reality. And, even if these premises and claims were true, it is highly unlikely that local governments would be any more eager to cooperate with their central cities (and even other suburbs) over these issues than they are now. One of many reasons for this may be, as Swanstrom (1996, 2001) has observed, that the New Regionalism places too much reliance on an economic justification for regional cooperation and lacks a sufficient understanding of politics. And, it is politics that fundamentally determines whether, to what extent, and over what issues local governments in regions cooperate.

According to Frisken and Norris (2001) the New Regionalist economic argument, which is central to its very being, "… assumes not only that it is in the economic self-interest of local governments operating in city regions to overcome their divisions, but also that the economic imperative (i.e., the need to be competitive globally) will impel them to do so …" (468). The reality, however, is quite different. Because it is not in their self-interest to do so (as they perceive their self-interests), local governments in American regions largely do not cooperate in order to address the negative externalities of fragmentation and sprawl or to ensure that their regions more effectively compete in the global economy.

Thus, in terms of its effectiveness, the New Regionalism might as well be the old regionalism redux, albeit with slightly different flavoring. Finally, for reasons that I will discuss in some detail in the concluding chapter, it is highly doubtful that the New Regionalism will be any more successful in the future than it is now in achieving its objective of metropolitan governance through voluntary cooperation.

References

Blair, John P. and Zhongcai Zhang. 1994. Ties that bind reexamined. *Economic Development Quarterly*, 8(4): 373–377.

Bradbury, Katharine L., Anthony Downs and Kenneth A. Small. 1982. *Urban Decline and the Future of American Cities.* Washington, DC: Brookings Institution.

Brenner, Neil. 2002. Decoding the newest "metropolitan regionalism" in the USA: A critical overview. *Cities*, 19(1): 3–21.

Danielson, Michael N. 1976. *The Politics of Exclusion.* New York: Columbia University Press.

Dye, Thomas R., Charles S. Liebman, Oliver P. Williams and Harold Herman. 1963. Differentiation and cooperation in a metropolitan area. *Midwest Journal of Political Science*, 7(2): 145–155.

Downs, Anthony. 1992. *Stuck in Traffic: Coping with Peak Hour Traffic Congestion.* Washington, DC: Brookings Institution.

Downs, Anthony. 1994. *New Visions for Metropolitan America.* Washington, DC: Brookings Institution and Lincoln Land Institute.

Downs, Anthony and Robert Puentes. 2005. The need for regional anticongestion policies. In Bruce Katz and Robert Puentes (eds), *Taking the High Road: A Metropolitan Agenda for Transportation Reform.* Washington, DC: Brookings Institution Press.

Feiock, Richard C. 2007. Rational choice and regional governance. *Journal of Urban Affairs*, 29(1): 47–63.

Frisken, Frances and Donald F. Norris. 2001. Regionalism reconsidered. *Journal of Urban Affairs*, 23(5): 467–78.

Garreau, Joel. 1991. *Edge City: Life on the New Frontier.* New York: Anchor Books.

Hanlon, Bernadette and Thomas J. Vicino. 2007. The Fate of Inner Suburbs: Evidence from Metropolitan Baltimore. *Urban Geography*, 28(3): 249–275.

Harrigan, John, J and Ronald K. Vogel. 2007. *Political Change in the Metropolis* (8th ed.). New York: Pearson-Longman.

Hawkins, Christopher V. 2010. Competition and cooperation: Local government joint ventures for economic development. *Journal of Urban Affairs*, 32(2): 253–275.

Hill, Edward W., Harold L. Wolman and Coit Cook Ford. 1995. Can suburbs survive without their central cities: Examining the suburban dependency hypothesis. *Urban Affairs Review*, 31(2): 147–174.

Kantor, Paul. 2000. Can regionalism save poor cities? Politics, institutions, and interests in Glasgow. *Urban Affairs Review*, 35(6): 794–820.

Kantor, Paul. 2006. Regionalism and reform: A comparative perspective on Dutch urban politics. *Urban Affairs Review*, 41(6): 800–829.

Kantor, Paul, Christian Lefevre, Asato Saito, H.V. Savitch and Andy Thornley. 2012. *Struggling Giants: City-Region Governance in London, New York, Paris and Tokyo.* Minneapolis, MN: University of Minnesota Press.

Lackowska, Marta. 2007. Metropolitan governance in Poland: Is voluntary cooperation condemned to failure? In Jan Erling Klausen and Pawel Swianiewicz, *Cities in City Regions. Governing the Diversity*. Warsaw: University of Warsaw, Faculty of Geography and Regional Studies.

Lackowska, Marta and Donald F. Norris. 2014. *Metropolitan Governance (Or not!) in Poland and the United States.* A paper presented at the 2014 annual conference of the European Urban Research Association. June 19–21. Paris, France.

Ledebur, Larry C. and William R. Barnes. 1992. *Metropolitan Disparities and Economic Growth: City Distress and the Need for a Federal Growth Package.* Washington DC: National League of Cities.

Ledebur, Larry C. and William R. Barnes. 1993. *All in it Together: Cities, Suburbs, and Local Economic Regions.* Washington, DC: National League of Cities.

Lovering, John. 1999. Theory led by policy: The inadequacies of the "New Regionalism." *International Journal of Urban and Regional Research*, 23(2): 379–395.

Norris, Donald F. 2001a. Whither metropolitan governance? *Urban Affairs Review*, 36(4): 532–550.

Norris, Donald F. 2001b. Prospects for regional governance under the New Regionalism: Economic imperatives versus political impediments. *Journal of Urban Affairs*, 23(5): 557–571.

Olberding. Julia C. 2002. Does regionalism beget regionalism? The relationship between norms and regional partnerships for economic development. *Public Administration Review*, 62(4): 480–491.

Orfield, Myron. 1997 (paperback in 1998). *Metropolitics: A Regional Agenda for Community and Stability.* Washington, DC: Brookings Institution.

Post, Stephanie Shirley and Robert M. Stein. 2000. State economies, metropolitan governance, and urban-suburban economic dependence. *Urban Affairs Review*, 36(1): 46–60.

Pressman, Jeffrey L. and Aaron Wildavsky. 1984. *Implementation: How Great Expectations in Washington arc Dashed in Oakland.* Oakland, CA: University Of California Press.

Rusk, David. 1993. *Cities without Suburbs.* Washington, DC: Woodrow Wilson Center Press.

Sancton, Andrew. 2001. Canadian cities and the New Regionalism. *Journal of Urban Affairs*, 23(5): 543–555.

Savitch, H.V., David Collins, Daniel Sanders and John P. Markham. 1993. Ties that bind: central cities, suburbs, and the new metropolitan region. *Economic Development Quarterly.* 7(4): 341–57.

Savitch, H.V. and Ronald K. Vogel. 2000. Introduction: Paths to New Regionalism. In H.V. Savitch and Ronald K. Vogel (eds), Symposium on the new regionalism and its policy agenda. *State and Local Government Review*, 32(3): 158–68.

Swanstrom, Todd. 1996. Ideas matter: reflections on the new regionalism. *Cityscape: A Journal of Policy Development and Research*, 2(2): 5–21.

Swanstrom, Todd. 2001. What we argue about when we argue about regionalism. *Journal of Urban Affairs*, 23(5): 479–496.

Thompson, Lyke. 1997. *The interlaced metropolis: Cities in layered networks and confederations in the Detroit Urbanized area.* Detroit, MI: College of Urban, Labor and Metropolitan Affairs, Wayne State University. Unpublished paper.

Vicino, Thomas J. 2008. The spatial transformation of first-tier suburbs, 1970 to 2000: The case of metropolitan Baltimore. *Housing Policy Debate*, 19(3): 479–518.

Voith, Richard 1992. City and suburban growth: substitutes or complements? *Business Review*, September/October, 21–33.

Walker, David B. 1987. Snow White and the 17 dwarfs: From metro cooperation to governance. *National Civic Review*, 76(1): 14–28.

Weir, Margaret, Harold Wolman and Todd Swanstrom. 2005. The calculus of coalitions: Cities. suburbs and the metropolitan agenda. *Urban Affairs Review*, 40(6): 730–760.

Wheeler, Stephen M. 2002. The New Regionalism: Key characteristics of an emerging movement. *Journal of the American Planning Association*, 68(3): 267–278.

Williams, Oliver. 1967. Lifestyle values and political decentralization in metropolitan areas. *Southwest Social Science Quarterly*, 48(4): 299–310.

Chapter 5

Metropolitan Governance Survey

In this chapter, I present the results of a nationwide survey of metropolitan governance and cooperation that I conducted in 2012–2013. I conducted the survey among the Councils of Government, Regional Planning Agencies and equivalent organizations (hereinafter referred to as COGs) in the 102 largest metropolitan areas in the US. These were the COGs serving regions with populations of 500,000 or greater.

The purpose of the survey was to enable me to better understand whether, and the extent to which, local governments in these metropolitan areas engage in governance, and whether, and the extent to which, those local governments cooperate with one another to address common problems and issues in their metropolitan areas. I conducted the survey with the support of Mr. Fred Abouselman (then Director) and his staff at the National Association of Regional Councils (NARC), the representative body of regional organizations. I partnered with NARC to ensure that the survey instrument best captured the issues of governance and cooperation in metropolitan areas and also to ensure the highest possible response rate to the survey.

In the summer and fall of 2012, I developed a draft survey instrument and shared it with Mr. Abouselman and his staff. After receiving feedback from them as well as from colleagues in the field, I finalized the instrument. During November of 2012, I sent formal invitations via the US mail to the executive directors (or their equivalents) of the 102 selected COGs, inviting them to participate in the survey. I followed the letters with emails containing a link to the survey instrument on Survey Monkey. Subsequently, I followed up with additional emails and telephone calls, as needed, to COGs that had not completed the survey. When I closed the survey in February 2013, I had received completed responses from 43 COGs, constituting a response rate of 42.2 percent. For social science research of this type, such a response rate is considered very good.

Even with such a response rate, I was concerned about the representativeness of the respondents. Here, I chose to employ the variable size, as measured by population, to test representativeness. This is a common variable often used by local government scholars to determine if survey respondents are representative of overall groups of governments (for example, Norris and Kraemer, 1996; Norris and Reddick, 2013).

I found that the responding organizations were reasonably, although not perfectly, representative by population (Table 5.1). To begin with, the overall sample of 102 COGs included far more small regions (small defined as populations

80   *Metropolitan Governance in America*

between 500,000 and one million) than medium sized (defined as populations between one and two million) or large regions (defined as regions with populations greater than two million). This should not be surprising since the US has far more small and medium-sized local governments than large ones (ICMA, 2013). Nearly half of the 102 COGS represented small metro areas (49 or 48 percent). Medium-sized regions accounted for nearly a quarter (24 or 23.5 percent) of the overall sample, and large COGs accounted for nearly three in ten (29 or 28.5 percent).

The responding COGs were much more balanced in terms of population. Slightly over one third (16 or 37.2 percent) were from large metro areas. Just slightly over one-quarter (12 or 27.9 percent) were from medium-sized regions, and about one-third (15 or 34.9 percent) were from small regions. While this is not perfect representativeness, it is certainly close enough to give us confidence that none of the three groups of respondents dominated or drove the survey results.

Table 5.1   Response rate and representativeness

	N in Sample		N of Responses	
Population	No.	%	No.	%
Small	49	48.0	15	34.9
Medium	24	23.5	12	27.9
Large	29	28.5	16	37.2
Region				
North central	19	18.6	13	30.2
Northeast	20	19.6	6	14.0
South	40	39.2	20	46.5
West	23	22.6	4	9.3

Region of the country is another common variable used by local government scholars to help determine sample representativeness. Region is useful for analytical purposes because scholars have noted regional variations in a number of local government characteristics and policy choices (for example, Norris and Kraemer, 1996: Norris and Reddick, 2013). By this measure, however, representativeness was considerably challenged. Here, nearly half of responding COGs (20 or 46.5 percent) were from the southern region of the US, and nearly one-third (13 or 30.2 percent) were from the north central region. Only one in seven (6 or 14.0 percent) were from the northeast and only one in ten (4 or 9.3 percent) were from the west.[1]

---

1   Extenuating circumstances may have contributed to the low response rate among COGs in the northeast. In October 2012, Super Storm Sandy hit the East Coast, with New

Metropolitan Governance Survey

This suggests that readers should be somewhat cautious when interpreting the results of the survey. This is so because of possible biases introduced to survey results due to the dominance of two regions (and the absence of a substantial numbers of respondents from two other regions).

Survey Results

In the remainder of this chapter, I discuss the results of the survey. The survey instrument included questions about the existence and operation of metropolitan governance and cooperation, whether regions boasted formal units of governance or cooperation, how widespread were governance and cooperation, the types of functions and services around which governance and cooperation occur, whether governance and cooperation included non-governmental as well as governmental organizations, and the effectiveness (or lack thereof) of governance and cooperation. I begin with survey results from questions about metropolitan governance and follow with survey results from questions about metropolitan cooperation.

Metropolitan Governance

I provided respondents with my definitions of metropolitan governance and cooperation (see Chapter 1). These definitions appeared in the survey instrument immediately prior to the sections that contained questions about metropolitan governance and cooperation, respectively. I intended the definitions to provide guidance to respondents about my meaning of these terms. As such, all respondents operated (in theory at least) from a common definition of metropolitan governance and cooperation in answering the survey.

I defined metropolitan governance as:

> The formal association of governments, non-governmental organizations and/ or residents in a metropolitan area for the purpose of controlling or regulating behavior and/or performing functions or services within the metropolitan area. Governance is areawide, governing decisions are binding, and participants can be compelled to comply with them.

The first question in the instrument asked whether metropolitan governance occurred in the metro area encompassed by a COG. Most respondents (32 or 74.4 percent) said that governance did not occur in their regions. However, a small minority (11 or 25.6 percent) responded that governance did occur.

Jersey and New York sustaining the most severe damage. COGs in both New Jersey and New York informed me that they were unable to participate in the survey because of the impact of Sandy.

I found these responses difficult to fathom. This is because it is well known in the urban affairs literature that, among the 381 metro areas in the nation, metropolitan governance arguably occurs in only two—Portland, OR and Minneapolis-St. Paul, MN. (However, such governance does not occur across the entirety of either region because the regional organizations in each encompass only a sub-set of the jurisdictions in their Census Bureau defined metropolitan areas.)

Thus, I reviewed the 11 completed survey instruments. In doing so, I discovered another oddity. In answering a later question in the instrument (question 13), some respondents indicated that governance occurred over services and functions that rarely if ever experience governance (often not even cooperation) in metropolitan America. These services included k-12 education, land use planning, zoning, public housing, among others. These are among the classic *lifestyle* issues over which local governments often engage in conflict rather than cooperation because these are functions over which local governments hardly ever surrender even a modicum of their control or autonomy.

In addition, another 29 respondents reported at least some level of governance around certain services and functions. These respondents said that governance did not occur in their metro area on question 1, yet said that governance occurred around specific services on question 13. In some cases, this may have occurred as a result of survey fatigue as respondents were trying to complete the survey and may have overlooked or by question 13 may have forgotten the definition of governance given at the start of the survey. In other cases, I suspect that this happened as in the case of the 11 that initially indicated governance to question 1 because they focused on what I later determined to be governance but at the sub-regional level.

I then contacted all of the respondents who answered yes to the existence of metro governance across their regions or to governance over some function or service either by phone or email (sometimes both) to confirm their answers. My discussions with them, in which I clarified the meaning of the term metropolitan governance and cleared up any other questions that the respondents had about the survey, resulted in each respondent agreeing that, under my definition (formal, areawide, regulatory, binding and coercive), metropolitan governance did not occur within their regions.

My discussions also revealed what I believe are reasons that may account for why these respondents initially said that governance did occur. First, all of the COGs that responded affirmatively on the question of metro governance were Metropolitan Planning Organizations (MPOs) under federal transportation funding law (SAFETEA_LU). That law establishes the procedures under which regional planning for federal transportation funding must occur. Every region in the country that wants to receive federal transportation funding must establish an MPO. The MPO, in turn—that is to say the jurisdictions that constitute the MPO—must develop and agree upon a plan (really a request) for federal transportation dollars. If the work of an MPO in this instance can be viewed as authoritative, then, under my definition, metropolitan governance would likely be served.

However, in all cases, the territories covered by these MPOs differ from their Census Bureau-defined metropolitan areas. Thus, while governance might otherwise be a reasonable term to use to describe the MPO's conduct of transportation planning in these regions, since none of the MPOs covered all of the Census Bureau-defined metropolitan area, metropolitan governance cannot be said to have occurred.

Instead, I would label this sub-regional governance and, throughout this study, I discovered many examples of sub-regional governance over various services and functions, a subject to which I will return in due course. This finding should not surprise anyone because of the long history of intergovernmental cooperation in the US. However, to my knowledge, this has not heretofore been reported in the regionalism literature.

There is also room for argument about whether MPOs actually engage in governance at all in the transportation planning process. First, it can be argued that MPOs engage in little more than a form of externally induced (induced, that is, by the promise of federal funding) cooperation. Second, an important criticism of MPOs is that they are more likely to look out for local interests than regional interests and, that in comparison to state Departments of Transportation and local governments that constitute the MPOs, the latter are relatively weak (Mallett, 2010; Vogel and Nezelkewicz, 2002). Such cooperation as exists in the regional transportation planning process, then, can resemble log-rolling, in which member jurisdictions make sure that they get as much of the transportation funding pie as possible for their own, not the region's needs. They do so in concert with other local governments through an "I'll support your request now if you have to support mine in the next round" sort of behavior. This way nearly everyone's pet projects are included at some point in the funding process. None of the parties gets everything they want, but no one starves.

Third, scholars have found that the composition of MPOs plays a role in the types of plans for federal transportation funding that these organizations adopt. MPOs dominated by elected officials tend to adopt plans that are more locally focused while those with more non-elected officials tend to adopt plans with more of a regional focus (Gerber and Gibson, 2009). Additionally, a greater number of voting members from suburban jurisdictions results in funding priorities increasingly shifting from transit and to highways (Nelson et al., 2004). And yet others have found that MPOs vary considerably in their ability to address regional versus local needs (Goetz et al., 2002). Thus, in at least some MPOs, transportation plans may resemble more of a cobbling together of the funding requests of the individual jurisdictions that constitute an MPO than true regional planning Although this book is not the proper place for a debate over the "planning" behavior of local governments in MPOs, these findings suggest a certain caution when imputing "governance" to the actions of MPOs around transportation planning.

Fourth, in any event, MPOs' plans must first be approved by their respective state departments of transportation and, ultimately, the US Department of Transportation (US DOT)—two higher authorities. And, the entire process operates under federal law so that, at the end of the day, federal law is authoritative and prevails in this process. What US DOT approves is what the local governments in a region must accept. The MPO request prior to state and ultimately US DOT action (that is, the MPO "plan") is not authoritative. It is merely a request.

Last, another reason why at least some COGs responded as they did about governance can be found in state law (at least in some states). Here, state law determines the legal catchment areas for various functions involving metropolitan governance and cooperation. As I noted above, MPOs are not always coterminous with Census Bureau-defined metro areas, and state law often determines those boundaries. States also carve out different geographies for other functions as well, including but not limited to regional land use planning, storm water management, air and water pollution control and more. Thus, it is clear that the boundaries of many "regions" across the nation may or may not be consistent with Census Bureau-defined metro areas. Actions of local governments within various regions might constitute a form of sub-regional governance, providing that it is regulatory, binding and coercive within that sub-regional territory. However, because those actions are not metro-wide, they do not constitute metro governance.

At least some of the COG directors with whom I spoke considered that city–county interactions over certain services and functions to be metro governance. It is well known in the literature that many central cities and their surrounding counties and/or surrounding suburbs engage in anywhere from a few to a wide range of cooperative activities, including activities that are informal and legally binding (governance). An unknown but probably non-trivial number of other central cities, central counties and suburbs, however, would rather fight than work together. But for current purposes I focus on cooperation.

Typical services and functions around which central cities and counties often cooperate include such things as arts and cultural districts and funding, business and economic development, emergency preparedness, public transit, transportation planning (as noted above), water and wastewater services and more, mainly though not exclusively systems maintenance functions. While city–county governance and/ or cooperation over issues of mutual interest are commendable, unless the metro area consists of a single central city and a single county, they do not constitute metropolitan governance by my definition. This is because the region includes only a subset of jurisdictions. In larger metro areas with multiple jurisdictions, the fact that two jurisdictions engage in governance activities can hardly be said to address areawide problems or issues—a key component of metropolitan governance.

As a result of my conversations and/or emails with the directors of these 40 COGs (11 that initially said governance occurred in their regions and 29 whose responses contained some anomalies) and for the reasons I discussed above, I concluded that metropolitan governance does not occur in any of the responding metropolitan areas, at least according to my definition. I also concluded that governance can and does occur at the sub-regional level, may include from a few to a large number of local governments and other actors, and may occur over a variety of services and functions.

I now turn to the second set of questions in the instrument that concerned metropolitan cooperation.

Metropolitan Cooperation

As indicated above, I provided my definition of metropolitan cooperation in the survey instrument immediately prior to the questions about this subject. I defined metropolitan cooperation as:

> The voluntary association of governments, non-governmental organizations and/or residents within a metropolitan area for purposes of addressing issues of mutual concern and/or performing functions and services. Cooperation may be areawide or may involve territory less than areawide. Cooperation may involve as few as two organizations or as many as all of the organizations in the area. Cooperation may involve one issue, function or service or many. Because cooperation is voluntary, decisions taken are not authoritative, and participants cannot be compelled to comply with them.

I first asked whether or not metropolitan cooperation occurred within metropolitan areas around the country. The overwhelming consensus (41 respondents or 95.3 percent) was that metropolitan cooperation did occur. Only two respondents (4.7 percent) indicated that cooperation did not occur (Table 5.2). It should not be surprising that nearly all of the COGs said that metropolitan cooperation occurred because of the vast literature in urban affairs that demonstrates that this is the case. Local communities in America have cooperated with one another over a wide array of issues since almost the beginning of the country.

Table 5.2   Does metropolitan governance occur in your metro area?

	Responses (n)	Percent
Yes	41	95.3
No	2	4.7
Total	43	100.0

What is surprising is that the directors of two COGs said that cooperation did not occur in their regions. According to one of the directors with whom I spoke, relations between the central city and its county were so toxic that cooperation between them was simply impossible. This finding may resonate in more than one or two regions in the nation. I can only speculate about why this might be the case, but it is also common knowledge in the field of urban affairs that some cities and counties and some cities and their suburbs just do not get along.

The survey then asked whether there were formal units or structures of metropolitan cooperation in these regions. Here, the great majority of respondents (27 or 87.1 percent) reported that formal units of cooperation existed in their metro areas, while four or 12.9 percent said that none existed (Table 5.3). Some examples include MPOs, COGs, arts and culture organizations, economic development organizations, joint library operations and joint emergency dispatch organizations.

Table 5.3   Do formal units of cooperation exist in your metro area?

	Responses (n)	Percent
Yes	27	87.1
No	4	12.9
Total	31	100.0

Next I asked, regardless of whether formal units existed, if cooperation was mostly formal or informal. By formal, I meant local governments working together through written agreements, contracts and the like. By informal, I meant working together in the absence of written agreements. I posed this question on a 10-point scale, with 1 meaning that cooperation was exclusively formal and 10 meaning it was exclusively informal. For purposes of this analysis, I grouped the responses as follows: 1–3 means mostly informal, 4–7 means it is mixed, and 8–10 means it is mostly formal (Table 5.4).

Table 5.4   Is cooperation mostly formal or informal?

	Responses (n)	Percent
Informal	9	21.4
Both	29	69.0
Formal	4	9.6
Total	42	100.0

Nearly seven in ten respondents (29 or 69.0 percent) said that cooperation occurred both formally and informally within their regions. Slightly more than one in five (nine or 21.4 percent) said that of cooperation was mostly informal, while about one in ten of the (four or 9.6 percent) said that cooperation was mostly formal. Because of the way I coded the data, Table 5.4 does not show the distribution of responses. Here, there was a substantial concentration of responses in the middle of the reporting scale. Nearly two-thirds (64 percent) of the COGs responded with answers in the 4–7 range. Ten percent in the 8–9 range (there were no 10s), and 22 percent in the 1–3 range.

Metropolitan Governance Survey 87

In addition to knowing whether cooperation was formal or informal, I wanted to learn how widespread it was (Table 5.5). I also asked this question on a 10-point scale with 1 meaning that there was no metropolitan cooperation and 10 meaning cooperation was widespread. For purposes of this analysis, I grouped the responses as follows: 1–3 means little or no cooperation; 4–7 means a moderate amount of cooperation; and 8–10 means widespread cooperation.

Table 5.5   How widespread is cooperation?

	Responses (n)	Percent
Not widespread	7	17.1
Moderately widespread	25	60.1
Very widespread	9	21.9
	41	100.0

A clear majority of COGs (25 or 60.1 percent) reported that there was a moderate amount of cooperation in their regions. Few of the COGs indicated that there was no cooperation (seven or 17.1 percent) or that cooperation was widespread (nine or 21.9 percent). Again, because of the way I coded the data, Table 5.5 does not show the distribution of responses. Here, there was also a substantial concentration of responses in the middle of the reporting scale. Sixty percent of the COGs responded with answers in the 4–7 range. Eighteen percent in the 2–3 range (there were no 1s) and 22 percent in the 8–10 range.

For nearly the past 50 years, urban scholars have distinguished between two different types of local government services and functions—*systems maintenance* and *lifestyle* (Williams, 1967). Typical systems maintenance functions include such things as water, sewer, solid waste, roads and streets, public transportation, infrastructure and the like. Typical lifestyle functions include such things as k-12 education, land use planning, zoning, land development control, policing, fire services, emergency medical services (EMS), code enforcement and the like.

Using this dichotomy, I asked if the functions and services that occurred under metropolitan cooperation were mainly systems maintenance or lifestyle. I defined these two types of functions in the survey instrument to provide all respondents with a common definition from which to operate when answering this question.

I posed this question on a 10-point scale, with 1 meaning exclusively systems maintenance and 10 meaning exclusively lifestyle. For purposes of this analysis, I grouped the responses as follows: 1–3 means mostly systems maintenance; 4–7 means a combination of systems maintenance and lifestyle; and 8–10 means mostly lifestyle (Table 5.6). Here, the great majority of respondents (32 or 80.0 percent) of respondents said that cooperation included a combination of both systems maintenance and limited lifestyle functions. Only eight or 20.0 percent

88　　　　　　　　　　*Metropolitan Governance in America*

said cooperation occurred mainly around systems maintenance functions, and none said it occurred mainly around lifestyle functions.

Table 5.6　Cooperation over systems maintenance or lifestyle functions

	Responses (n)	Percent
Systems Maintenance	8	20.0
Mixed	32	80.0
Lifestyle	0	0.0
Total	40	100.0

*　Responses 4 and 5 on the scale totaled 55 percent of COGs.

I next asked whether metro cooperation involved only local governments or whether it also included private sector and non-profit organizations. Once again I used a 10-point scale with 1 meaning that cooperation was exclusively governmental and 10 meaning that it always included private sector and non-profit organizations. For purposes of this analysis, I grouped the responses as follows: 1–3 means always or almost always governmental organizations; 4–7 means sometimes includes private sector and non-profit organizations; and 8–10 means always or nearly always includes private sector and non-profit organizations (Table 5.7).

Table 5.7　Organizations in cooperative ventures

	Responses	Percentage
Governmental only	12	29.2
Mixed	27	65.8
Private/public sector always	2	5.0
Total	41	100.0

Two-thirds (27 or 65.8 percent) said that cooperation included both private and non-profit sector organizations. Nearly three in ten of the COGs (12 or 29.2 percent) said that metro cooperation exclusively or nearly exclusively involved governmental organizations only. A very small minority (2 or 5 percent) said that metro cooperation always or nearly always included private and non-profit organizations (and none of these responses was a 9 or a 10 on my scale).

In addition to whether metro cooperation occurred in these regions, I wanted to know how effective the respondents felt it was in addressing negative externalities

Metropolitan Governance Survey 89

and areawide problems such as sprawl, fiscal and service inequities, traffic congestion, air and water pollution, and so on. Here, too, I again used a 10-point scale with 1 meaning cooperation is highly ineffective and 10 meaning highly effective. For purposes of this analysis, I grouped the responses as follows: 1–3 means largely or completely ineffective; 4–7 means somewhat effective; and 8–10 means effective or highly effective (Table 5.8).

Table 5.8   Effectiveness of metro cooperation

	Responses	Percentage
Ineffective	8	20.5
Moderately effective	30	77.0
Effective	1	2.5
Total	39	100.0

Slightly over three-quarters of the COGs (30 or 77.0 percent) said that cooperation was somewhat effective in addressing negative externalities and areawide problems. About one in five respondents (eight or 20.5 percent) said that metropolitan cooperation was completely or largely ineffective in their regions, while only a tiny minority (one or 2.5 percent) said that cooperation was largely or completely effective (and there were no responses of 9 or 10 on my scale).

What conclusions can be drawn from these data? First, local government cooperation occurred in nearly all metro areas in my sample. As I said earlier, this is not surprising—local governments in America have cooperated with one another along a variety of issues for hundreds of years. Nor is it particularly surprising that in some (albeit a few) regions local governments did not cooperate at all.

Second, although formal units of cooperation exist in most (87 percent) metro areas, local government cooperation is both formal (that is, it operates under written agreements) and informal (it operates in the absence of written agreements) in those regions. Third, most regions reported that cooperation was moderately widespread, with few reporting little or no cooperation and few reporting widespread cooperation.

Fourth, the great majority of COGs said that cooperation operated over both systems maintenance and lifestyle issues. This is somewhat at odds with the predominant view from the urban literature, which says that local governments are more likely (largely for political reasons) to cooperate over systems maintenance than lifestyle issues. Yet, none of the respondents said that cooperation occurred mainly around lifestyle issues, and most of the responses that said cooperation included both systems maintenance and lifestyle issues were in the 4–5 range on my scale. Only a few were in the 6–7 range. This lends at least a modicum of credibility to the predominant view from the literature.

90 *Metropolitan Governance in America*

Little research has been conducted about the extent to which private sector and non-profit organizations enter into cooperative arrangements with their regions' local governments. This survey provides some evidence to begin closing that gap in our knowledge. Thus, the fifth finding is the great majority of COGs said that metro cooperation in their regions sometimes included private and non-profit sector organizations. However, three in ten said that cooperation mainly included local governments, and none said it always included the private and non-profit sectors. Thus, while cooperation in metro areas sometimes includes private and non-profit organizations, it is skewed in the direction of the public sector.

Finally, the great majority of the respondents said that cooperation is moderately successful in addressing areawide problems and issues like sprawl, fiscal and service inequities, traffic congestion, air and water pollution and the like. Based on the overwhelming preponderance of literature on the negative externalities of metropolitan growth, I find it hard to believe that this can be true—that metropolitan cooperation is even moderately effective in addressing these externalities. Is there any evidence from that literature that tells us that any region in the US is making progress against them? Is it even remotely possible that cooperation (actions that are voluntary, non-binding, and cannot be enforced) is likely to address these and other externalities effectively if at all? I doubt it.

This, then, leads me to wonder why three-quarters of respondents said that cooperation was moderately effective in addressing them. While I have no direct evidence from the survey, I can offer a few educated guesses. First, I suspect that it would be very difficult for COG leaders to respond otherwise or they would be undermining the very *raison d'etre* of their organizations and, hence, their jobs. As a function of their jobs and their professional norms, COG directors may also be more optimistic about their regions' ability to address negative externalities than, say, cynical academics and journalists. Finally, a few COG directors told me that their responses were really about the effectiveness of their organizations on the issues that they were chartered to address. Thus, they were not responding about the effectiveness of intergovernmental cooperation in their regions to address these negative externalities.

Next I turn to cross-tabulations that I conducted to attempt to identify any relationships between the size of regions as measured by population and the metropolitan cooperation outcomes that I reported in the preceding section.

Levels of Governance and Cooperation by Population Size

Researchers have found that size often matters to local government adoption of innovations. Larger governments have typically been found to be earlier and greater adopters of various innovative policies and practices. Scholars reason that size (as measured by population) is a surrogate for such things as larger budgets, larger (and more sophisticated) staffs, and greater needs that, in turn, produce greater levels of adoption (for example, Norris and Kraemer, 1996).

As a result, I felt it would be worthwhile to examine whether size matters in relation to various aspects of metropolitan cooperation. That is, are differences in the size of regions systematically related to how local governments in those regions behave in terms of metropolitan cooperation? This would be an especially useful exercise, I reasoned, because the population range across the metropolitan area respondents to this survey is considerable, from a low of just above 500,000 (Durham-Chapel Hill, NC) to a high of 13 million (Los Angeles, CA). I coded the responding metro areas as follows: small (less than one million residents), medium (between one and two million), and large (more than two million).

I first examined whether size (population) mattered to whether metropolitan cooperation occurred. The answer is that it did not (Table 5.9). Here, either all or nearly all of respondents, regardless of size, reported that metropolitan cooperation occurred in their regions (14 or 93.3 percent of small regions; 11 or 91.7 of medium regions, and all of the large regions). Next, I turned to whether size mattered with regard to the existence of formal units or structures of cooperation (Table 5.10). Here, the answer is maybe. Although nearly all regions, regardless of size, reported that such units existed in their regions, there was a slight tilt in favor of large regions. Eight in ten (12 or 80.0 percent) of small regions reported formal units or structures; 10 or 90.9 percent of medium-sized regions did; and all large regions did.

Table 5.9   Size and metro cooperation

Cooperation	Yes No.	%	No No.	%
Small	14	93.3	1	6.7
Medium	11	91.7	1	8.3
Large	16	100	0	0.0
Total	41	95.4	2	4.7

Table 5.10   Size and formal units of cooperation

Formal Units of Cooperation	Yes No.	%	No No.	%
Small	12	80.0	3	20.0
Medium	10	90.9	1	9.1
Large	16	100.0	0	0
Total	38	90.5	4	9.5

92   *Metropolitan Governance in America*

Size appears to be substantially related to whether cooperation was mostly formal or informal in these metropolitan areas (Table 5.11). The larger the region, the more likely cooperation was to occur both formally and informally. Here, more than eight in ten COGs serving large regions (13 or 81.3 percent) reported that cooperation included a mixture of the formal and the informal, while none reported that cooperation was either mostly formal, and few said mostly informal (three or 18.75 percent). Among medium-sized regions, by contrast, three-quarters of the COGs (eight or 72.7 percent) reported that cooperation included a mixture of the formal and the informal, while only one (one or 9.1 percent) reported that cooperation was mostly informal and only two reported that it was mostly formal (18.2 percent). Finally, half (eight or 53.3 percent) of the COGs serving small regions reported that cooperation included a mixture of the formal and the informal, while only five (33.3 percent) reported that cooperation was mostly informal, and only two reported that it was mostly formal (13.3 percent).

Table 5.11   Size and formal or informal cooperation

Type of Cooperation	Mostly Informal		Mixed		Mostly Formal	
	No.	%	No.	%	No.	%
Small	5	33.3	8	53.3	2	13.3
Medium	1	9.1	8	72.7	2	18.2
Large	3	18.8	13	81.3	0	0.0

I also wanted to know if size was related to how widespread cooperation was in these regions and it appeared to be so (Table 5.12). The larger the region, the more likely cooperation was to be moderately widespread. Eight in ten (12 or 80.0 percent) of respondents in large metro areas reported that cooperation was moderately widespread and another two (13.3 percent) said it was very widespread (for a total of 93.3 percent). Two-thirds (seven or 63.6 percent) of COGs serving

Table 5.12   Size and how widespread is cooperation

Widespread Cooperation	Not Widespread		Mixed		Very Widespread	
	No.	%	No.	%	No.	%
Small	5	33.34	6	40.0	4	26.67
Medium	1	9.09	7	63.63	3	27.27
Large	1	6.67	12	80.0	2	13.33

Metropolitan Governance Survey 93

medium-sized regions said cooperation was widespread and another three (27.3 percent) said it was very widespread (for a total of 90.1 percent). By contrast, only four in ten (six or 40.0 percent) of small regions reported cooperation being moderately widespread, while four (26.7 percent) said it was very widespread (for a total of 66.7 percent). However, a third (five or 33.3 percent), said that there was little or no cooperation in their regions.

Next, I examined whether a relationship existed between size and the functions over which cooperation occurred, either systems maintenance or lifestyle (Table 5.13). COGs in large metro areas were substantially more likely to report that cooperation involved a mix of both system maintenance and lifestyle issues (14 or 93.3 percent) than COGs in either medium-sized (nine or 81.8 percent) or small (nine or 64.3 percent) metro areas. In somewhat of a mirror image, COGs representing small regions were more likely to report that cooperation was more systems maintenance-oriented (five or 35.7 percent) than either those in medium-sized metro areas (five or 18.2 percent), or large metros (two or 13.3 percent).

Table 5.13   Functions of cooperation

Functions of Cooperation	Mostly Systems Maintenance		Mixed		Mostly Lifestyle	
	No.	%	No.	%	No.	%
Small	5	35.7	9	64.3	0	0.0
Medium	2	18.2	9	81.8	0	0.0
Large	1	6.7	14	93.3	0	0.0

I then wanted to learn if a relationship existed between size and whether non-governmental organizations were included in metro cooperation (Table 5.14). Once again, size seemed to matter with larger regions reporting a greater degree of inclusion of private sector and non profit organizations in the cooperation mix. The great majority of respondents serving large metro areas (12 or 80.0 percent) reported that cooperation often included both local governments and private sector and non-profit organizations. Nearly three-quarters of COGs serving medium-sized metro areas (72.7 percent) said that cooperation included both governmental and private sector and non-profit organizations. Among small metro areas, fewer than half of respondents (seven or 46.7 percent) indicated that cooperation included a mix of governmental and private sector and non-profit organizations. More COGs serving small metro areas (seven or 46.7), followed by those serving medium-sized regions (three or 27.3), and those serving large regions (two or 13.3) said that cooperation was mostly or exclusively governmental. Finally, only two COGs, one serving a small and one a large region, said that cooperation always or nearly always included the private and non-profit sectors.

94 Metropolitan Governance in America

Table 5.14   Organizations in cooperative ventures

Partnership Types	Exclusively Governmental		Mixed		Always Includes Private and Non-Profit	
	No.	%	No.	%	No.	%
Small	7	46.67	7	46.67	1	6.67
Medium	3	27.27	8	72.73	0	0.0
Large	2	13.33	12	80.0	1	6.67

Finally, I wondered if a relationship existed between size and the COGs' perceptions of the effectiveness of metropolitan cooperation in addressing areawide problems and externalities. As the data in Table 5.15 show, there was very little difference among the responses to this question by population. Large majorities of all COGs said that cooperation was somewhat effective. A smaller but non-trivial fraction felt that cooperation was ineffective. Only one COG (representing a large region) responded that cooperation was more than moderately effective. However, on my scale of 1 to 10 (with 10 being highly effective), this respondent gave cooperation an 8, and none of the respondents ranked effectiveness a 9 or a 10.

Table 5.15   Effectiveness of cooperation

Effectiveness	Ineffective		Mixed		Effective	
	No.	%	No.	%	No.	%
Small	5	35.7	9	64.3	0	0.0
Medium	3	25.0	9	75.0	0	0.0
Large	3	18.8	12	75.0	1	6.25

I can draw at least the following conclusions from these findings. First, size was not associated with whether cooperation occurred in regions, whether formal units of cooperation existed in regions or perceptions of the effectiveness of cooperation to address the negative externalities of metropolitan development. Why might this be? Large majorities of the COGs said that cooperation occurred in their regions (95 percent) and that formal units of cooperation existed (87 percent). With majorities this great, one would not expect much, if any, variation among the responding units based on any single variable.

Regarding effectiveness, as I noted earlier, it is probably difficult for COG directors to say that cooperation is completely ineffective because of their occupational biases. As a result, the survey data showed only rather small differences among the COGs responses to this question.

These results show that size was, however, associated with whether cooperation is formal or informal, how widespread it was, whether it involved systems maintenance or lifestyle issues, and whether it included non-governmental actors. In these cases, I found that cooperation in regions with larger populations was more likely than in medium-sized or small regions to:

- include both formal and informal cooperation;
- be moderately widespread;
- include both systems maintenance and lifestyle issues; and
- be more inclusive of private sector and non-profit organizations.

What properties of large regions might be driving these differences? The data from this survey do not enable me to answer this question directly, but again I am able to make some educated guesses. The first is that because of their greater size and presumably greater number of actors, large regions may have both greater opportunities and greater flexibility when it comes to engaging in different forms of cooperation (formal as well as informal, governmental and non-governmental actors). Conversely, small regions may be relatively more constrained here—fewer opportunities, fewer actors and less flexibility. Second, it is likely that cooperation is more widespread in large versus small regions because the former serve larger territories, include a greater number (and presumably magnitude) of areawide problems to be addressed, and have a greater number of actors. Third, size may also explain the greater likelihood that cooperation includes both systems maintenance and lifestyle function again because of the larger territory and larger numbers of problems and actors. Large regions probably also have greater budgetary and staff capabilities to engage in cooperative actions. Of course, these are educated guesses, and I would suggest that the mechanisms of causality be at least one subject for further research into metropolitan cooperation.

Conclusion

The purpose of the survey reported in this chapter was to produce empirical data with which I could then ascertain whether local governments in US metropolitan areas engaged in governance and/or cooperation and the extent to which either or both occurred in those areas. The survey, which targeted the largest 102 metro areas in the US, received a 42.2 percent response rate, which is considered strong for social science research. Respondents were representative of regions by population, one variable often found to have a causal relationship to innovation adoption and policy transfer. Respondents were not representative by region of the country. However, this variable is not as strong a predictor of innovation adoption and policy transfer as population. Nevertheless, readers should be aware of this potential limitation to these data.

The data from the survey confirmed my initial assumption, which was based on my reading of the literature on this subject as well as with interviews over the years with local governmental officials. That assumption was that metropolitan governance does not occur in the United States. This result should (although it probably will not) put to rest an ongoing debate among urban scholars over regional governance. This survey found no evidence that metropolitan governance occurs in the US—at least by a carefully drawn and rigorous definition of governance. Moreover, as I will show in the concluding chapter of this book, there are compelling reasons to believe that not only does metropolitan governance not occur, but also that it probably cannot and will not occur.

The survey data also showed that metropolitan cooperation, not surprisingly, is widespread and includes both systems maintenance and lifestyle issues. This should not be a surprise since, after all, local governments in the US have been cooperating around a wide variety of issues ever since the beginning of the country. What is new from these data is the rather larger extent than expected of cooperation around lifestyle issues. This clearly deserves further research to understand why this is the case since it flies in the face of the conventional wisdom and extant scholarship about the types of issues around which local governments cooperate (for example, LeRoux and Carr, 2010).

Beyond metropolitan governance and cooperation, I also found that sub-regional governance occurs in many regions over a variety of issues and across a variety of sub-regional geographies. These data do not allow me to explain how, why or to what extent sub-regional cooperation occurs. This, too, should be the subject of future research metropolitan governance and cooperation, which should focus at least in part on the conditions under which sub-regional governance occurs and the functions and services around which it occurs. For example, does sub-regional governance occur because of greater or lesser degrees of fragmentation and sprawl? Does it vary by the population of regions, by other variables found to be associated with innovation adoption and policy transfer? Is sub-regional governance able to address the negative externalities of fragmentation and sprawl effectively? Further research on these and other questions about sub-regional governance is necessary and will enable scholars to better understand governance in metro areas that occurs below the regional level.

References

Gerber, Elisabeth, R. and Clark C. Gibson. 2009. Balancing regionalism and localism: How institutions and incentives shape American transportation policy. *American Journal of Political Science*, 53(3): 633–648.

Goetz, Andrew, Paul S. Dempsey and Carl Larson. 2002. Metropolitan Planning Organizations: Findings and recommendations for improving transportation planning. *Publius*, 32(1): 87–105.

International City/County Management Association. 2013. Inside the yearbook. *The Municipal Yearbook: 2013*. Washington, DC: Author (pp. ix–xviii).

LeRoux, Kelly, and Jered Carr. 2010. Prospects for centralizing services in an urban county: Evidence from eight self-organized networks of local public services. *Journal of Urban Affairs*. 32(4): 449–470.

Mallett, William J. 2010. *Metropolitan Transportation Planning*. Washington, DC: Congressional Research Service.

Nelson, Arthur C., Thomas W. Sanchez, James F. Wolf and Mary Beth Farquhar. 2004. Metropolitan Planning Organization voting structure and transit investment bias: Preliminary analysis and social equity implications. *Transportation Research Record*, No. 1895: 1–7. Washington DC: National Research Council.

Norris, Donald F. and Kenneth L. Kraemer. 1996. Mainframe and PC computing in American cities: Myths and realities. *Public Administration Review*, 56(6): 568–576.

Norris, Donald F. and Christopher G. Reddick. 2013. Local e-government in the United States: Transformation or incremental change? *Public Administration Review*, 73(1): 165–175.

Vogel, Ronald K. and Norman Nezelkewicz. 2002. Metropolitan Planning Organizations and the New Regionalism: The Case of Louisville. *Publius*, 32(1): 107–129.

Williams, Oliver. 1967. Lifestyle values and political decentralization in metropolitan areas. *Southwest Social Science Quarterly*, 48(4): 299–310.

Chapter 6

A Look at the Evidence

In this chapter, I examine the available evidence, paltry though it may be, regarding the adoption of meaningful metropolitan reform in the US since the end of the Second World War. By meaningful metropolitan reform, I mean reforms that would enable local governments in regions to address the tough, areawide issues that they find difficult or impossible to address alone.[1] These are the issues that motivated the Metro Reformers and the New Regionalists to devise the structural and non-structural alternatives that they thought would help local governments address areawide problems.

In examining the evidence, I employ David Walker's (1987) categorization of the major alternatives available to local government. Although most of these alternatives do little more than nibble around the edges of the tough areawide metro issue, a few have the potential to produce significant metropolitan reform capable of allowing local governments to more effectively grapple with these issues. Of course, the latter alternatives that have such a potential are incredibly difficult to adopt, and, consequently, very few of them have been adopted. Indeed, because so few of the more far-reaching reforms have been adopted, it strikes me as being palpably absurd to claim, as some urban scholars do today, that there is anything like metropolitan government or governance almost anywhere in the US.

Metro Reform Alternatives

In 1987, David Walker wrote an article for the National Civic Review that has been cited extensively in the metro governance literature. In this article, he discussed 17 alternative approaches to regional governance.[2] See Table 6.1. Walker presented his alternatives in order from the easiest (and, therefore, the least likely to be

---

1 As I have noted elsewhere, these are the problems most frequently cited by the Metro Reformers and New Regionalists. They are also the really tough, controversial issues around which local governments in metropolitan areas find meaningful cooperation quite difficult. They include: uncontrolled suburban growth; sprawl; governmental fragmentation; loss of open space; traffic congestion; air and water pollution; water supply and distribution; sanitation and solid waste; public education; lack of affordable housing; disparities in wealth, tax base, services and need; segregation by race and class; disinvestment in central cities and their decline; and occasionally others.

2 Note, however, that in the title to the table found on p. 16 of Walker's article, he entitled these alternatives service delivery, not governance.

100   *Metropolitan Governance in America*

able to address tough, controversial regional problems) to the most difficult (and, therefore, the least likely to be adopted).[3] He considered the first eight as the easiest to adopt, the next six as the middling alternatives in terms of adoption likelihood and the final three the most difficult to adopt. I adhere to his categorization.

Table 6.1   Regional approaches to service delivery

Regional Approaches to Service Delivery
Easiest
1. Informal cooperation
2. Interlocal service agreements
3. Joint powers agreements
4. Extraterritorial powers
5. Regional councils/councils of government
6. Federally encouraged single-purpose districts
7. State planning and development districts
8. Contracting (private)
Middling
9. Local special districts
10. Transfer of functions
11. Annexation
12. Regional special districts and authorities
13. Metro multi-purpose district
14. Reformed urban county
Hardest
15. One-tier consolidation
16. Two-tier consolidation
17. Three-tier reforms

Source: David Walker, 1987, 'Snow White and the 17 dwarfs: From metro cooperation to governance,' *National Civic Review*, 76(1):16.

The easy eight

First, there is voluntary cooperation. Not much needs to be said about this option because it is available to nearly all local governments nearly everywhere, nearly all the time, over nearly every issue imaginable. The problem is that, for the most part, local governments do not want to cooperate over the tough, controversial issues that metropolitan areas face. Nor do local governments want to relinquish their autonomy, which is almost essential if those governments are to be able to effectively address areawide problems.

---

3   Readers will recall from Chapter 2 that the ACIR (1973) noted the inverse correlation between the ease of adoption of Metro Reforms and their likelihood to address the tough issues.

A Look at the Evidence

Finally, voluntary cooperation is not a substitute for metropolitan governance because it suffers from the problem of the lowest common denominator (Norris, 2001a). The lowest common denominator (that is, the local government least willing to cooperate) would have the power either to not participate in or even to veto cooperative decisions. In the absence of the power to compel compliance, the least common denominator would prevail in any controversial issue or contested decision.

This means that local governments cannot be forced to cooperate voluntarily; not all local governments in a region are likely to be willing to cooperate over certain, if not all, of the tough, controversial issues; and, at any time, a local government that has agreed to cooperate voluntarily can withdraw from the cooperative venture. As I have noted previously, many scholars, including some of the notable Metro Reformers, have seen that voluntary cooperation is the weakest arrow in the quiver of metro governance.

Walker's second option is the interlocal service agreement. These, too, are voluntary between and among local governments in the sense that no one can be forced into such an agreement. However, once they are signed they have the force of law and partners in them can be compelled to perform, at least for as long as the agreement is in force. A well-known example here is the Lakewood Plan in California. Since the 1950s, municipalities in Los Angeles County have been able to contract with the county for various services in order to avoid having to produce those services in-house. Interlocal service agreements are mostly between two governments, such as a city and a county. More difficult to find, however, are cases of multiple local governments entering into service agreements. In any event, interlocal agreements are rarely able to address the tough and controversial issues that require areawide attention—for many of the same reasons that voluntary cooperation does not address these issues.

Third in difficulty of adoption is the joint powers agreement. These are similar to interlocal contracts but with one major exception. They are not examples of one government simply contracting with another for delivery of a service. Rather, joint powers agreements involve the formal agreement among two or more governments "... for the joint planning, financing and delivery of a service for the citizens of all the jurisdictions involved" (Walker, 1987: p. 17). According to a 2007 report of the Senate Local Government Committee of the California State Legislature, "Joint powers are exercised when the public officials of two or more agencies agree to create another legal entity or establish a joint approach to work on a common problem, fund a project, or act as a representative body for a specific activity" (Cypher and Grinnell, 2007: p. 5).

The report noted that nearly all governmental organizations in the state could legally enter into joint powers agreements, including agreements with federal agencies and governments in other states. Areas in which joint powers agreements were common in California included: managing groundwater, street and highway construction, transportation projects conservation efforts, airports, redevelopment projects, construction of various public facilities, delivering educational programs, managing benefits services for employee, insurance coverage, and more. Finally, the report observed that joint powers agreements are quite flexible and can be used in "almost any situation that benefits from public agencies' cooperation" (6).

Therein, of course, lies perhaps the greatest weaknesses of joint powers agreements. Local governments have to be willing to voluntarily engage in them, and, again, voluntary cooperation is very limited in its ability to address the really tough areawide issues.

This is followed, fourth, by extraterritorial powers or the ability of a municipal government to exercise control over certain functions, typically if not always, in unincorporated territory outside of their boundaries. The principal area in which extraterritorial power is exercised is in land development, particularly planning, zoning and subdivision development. Extraterritorial powers are especially important for municipalities in states that permit annexation of unincorporated territory because it allows the municipality to make sure that growth in these areas occurs in a manner that is consistent with the municipality's master plan and its zoning and subdivision regulations. The existence of extraterritorial powers and their specific extent and limitations is set by state law and varies across the country. Some states provide extensive extra territorial authority to their cities while others grant no such powers.

Most cities in North Carolina, for example, especially those with populations of 2,500 or more, exercise this authority, with larger cities using extraterritorial powers more than smaller ones. A city's extraterritorial area is limited by its population. Smaller cities (less than 10,000 in population) can exercise extraterritorial power up to one mile beyond their borders. With approval of their counties, larger cities can exercise this power up to two miles (between 10,000 and 25,000 in population) or three miles (larger than 25,000) beyond their borders. A 2005 survey showed that the great majority of North Carolina cities, however, exercised this power only within one mile of their borders (Owens, 2014).

In fifth place, Walker named Regional Councils, Councils of Government (COGs) and similar entities. I am not sure that I would concur that COGs are of much value today in addressing the challenging areawide problems in metropolitan America (with one exception, that is). COGs certainly are not a place to go to find metropolitan governance. This is borne out in the results of the survey reported in Chapter 5.

Today, COGS receive virtually no support for areawide planning and coordination from the federal government, unlike the modest support that they once received prior to the presidency of Ronald Reagan. Few COGs provide services within or across regions, and the functions that they perform are largely of an advisory or technical assistance nature.

The exception to this is when COGs are also metropolitan planning organizations (MPOs) under federal transportation legislation (most recently P.L. 112–141, the Moving Ahead for Progress in the 21st Century Act or MAP-21, adopted in the summer of 2012).[4] In this role, along with their constituent units of government, the COGs engage in regional planning for federal transportation funding. Since federal funding is crucial in all regions for building and maintaining transportation infrastructure and to support public transport, one could argue that in this instance, COGs really do address an important and often controversial areawide problem. Moreover, when their constituent governments empower MPOs to engage in sound regional transportation planning, they are able to develop plans that arguably can be said to effectively address areawide needs. However, when the local governments that constitute an MPO act more like the political animals that they are (and less like rational, areawide planners) and cobble together a plan in order to maximize their respective shares of available federal dollars, they ignore both rational planning principles and areawide needs.

Last, COGs are purely voluntary and, as such, suffer from two critical weaknesses. Their membership typically consists of a set or subset of local governments in regions, which, in turn, control what the COGs can do. Therefore, controversial areawide issues rarely find their way onto COGs' agendas. As a county executive in the Baltimore, MD region once told me, the members of the Baltimore Metropolitan Council (the region's COG) will address anything that they can agree on, but they won't take up matters on which they cannot reach agreement. A second limitation, of course, is the least common denominator phenomenon.

Nevertheless, COGs are justified today, at least by some observers (myself included), for two principal reasons. First, they constitute the principal and in some regions the sole venue in which local government officials can meet, discuss issues of common concern and try to take mutual action on those concerns. Second, as noted above, many, although certainly not all, COGs are MPOs and, thus, they perform an important function for their member jurisdictions—that of securing federal funding for transportation funding. Beyond these reasons, COGs may also perform or facilitate certain functions for their member jurisdictions, such as acting as data repositories, performing certain types of analyses for a region as a whole or for member jurisdictions, geographic information systems (GIS) and mapping, and a variety of planning activities among others.

However, the fact remains that few COGs have much, if any, independent power. Moreover, because they must keep their member jurisdictions happy (again, see the lowest common denominator phenomenon), they have little or no ability to compel their members to comply with decisions jointly made. Thus, COGs are not likely to be any more effective in addressing the tough issues that regions face than voluntary cooperation.

Walker considered federally encouraged single-purpose regional bodies as the sixth of the easiest alternatives. These entities were required when strings were attached to various federal funding programs in the 1960s and early 1970s. Walker noted that by 1977 between 1,400 and 1,700 of them existed. However, by the late

---

4 MAP 21 is the linear successor to earlier federal transportation funding laws, known in the vernacular as TEA 21 and ISTEA, SAFETEA and SAFETEA–LU.

104   *Metropolitan Governance in America*

1980s (after the Reagan revolution in intergovernmental relations), hardly any of them remained, and these included "only in a few Federal aid programs (notably metro transportation" (Walker, 1987: p. 19). Because of the substantial withdrawal of the federal government from most of urban and regional affairs, little has changed for the better since Walker wrote this work. Hence, this alternative is really no longer an option for local governments to address areawide problems.

State planning and development districts were Walker's seventh alternative. These were entities established by state governments "... during the late 1960s and early 1970s to bring order to the chaotic proliferation of Federal special purpose regional programs" (19). Even today, a number of states have entities that are called state planning and/or development districts and they provide a range of functions, though mostly in the area of economic development. I would be inclined to remove these from Walker's list because they are really state initiatives, requiring state legislation and state government participation. Moreover, as Walker noted "... state purposes and goals are involved and the establishment of new statewide districting systems can at least initially appear threatening, especially to counties" (20). It seems to me quite unlikely that local government in metro areas would rush to join state-mandated districts in which state governments essentially determine the character and content of the districts.

Last among the easy eight, Walker named contracting with the private sector. Like voluntary cooperation, contracting with the private sector is available to nearly all local governments, nearly all the time and over nearly all functions and services. However, Walker correctly noted that enabling legislation may be needed and that public sector unions may oppose contracting out, thus making it somewhat more difficult to adopt than the previous seven alternatives.

Contracting with the private sector is generally limited to service provision (for example, trash collection, water and sewer services, and so on). This option is rarely if ever employed to address tough, controversial regional issues that have so concerned metropolitan reformers. Contracting with the private sector also suffers from many of the same limitations as voluntary cooperation, mainly because local governments have to voluntarily enter into contracts and can relatively easily withdraw from them.

The middling six

Next is what Walker called the middling six alternatives. These are more difficult to adopt than the easy eight, but are also somewhat more likely to be able to address the tough areawide problems facing metro areas. The first of these is the special district. Special districts are units of government, usually established by the action of general-purpose local governments (for example, cities, counties, townships) in order to provide a service or services that single local governments alone could not provide (water and wastewater are good examples, but there are many others). More often than not special districts provide a single function or service, overlap the boundaries of two or more local governments and are directed by appointed rather than elected officials (and, therefore, are more difficult to hold accountable). According to the 2012 Census of Governments, there were 38,266 special districts in the US.

The existence of special districts as a service delivery alternative in metro areas is both a blessing and a bane. They are a blessing because they enable local governments in metro areas to address at least some of the areawide problems that have arisen due to the growth and fragmentation of those areas. As the Metro Reformers and the ACIR knew, special districts are also a bane precisely because they enable local governments to address some areawide problems. In doing so, special districts undercut the need for areawide governance mechanisms and further fragment regions.

Local governments use them to *muddle through*, and muddling through provides the appearance that a more rational approach to metro governance (as preferred by the Metro Reformers) isn't necessary.

The second middling alternative is the transfer of functions. This allows cities and counties to transfer functions up, down and laterally. That is, counties can shift functions to cities and vice versa. Cities can transfer functions to other cities as well, although this is somewhat rare. Finally, local governments can transfer functions to their states. And all can transfer functions to special districts. This option is especially desirable to older, less well-off central cities because it enables them to off-load expensive functions, thus freeing up needed funds in the municipal budget.

To provide just one example, over the years the financially beleaguered City of Baltimore, Maryland, has transferred several functions and services to state government: port, airport, mass transit, the city jail, the city community college, a state–city are in a partnership to fund and operate the city's public school system as well as providing in one form or another about one-third of the city's budget.[5]

It is unclear, however, whether or the extent to which transferring functions is actually able to address areawide problems. This is because most metro areas, certainly those of any size, consist of multiple general and special-purpose local governments. And while a single city might get some relief by transferring functions to its county, for example, large-scale transfers across jurisdictional boundaries, especially among multiple counties, do happen. Further, as is the case with special districts, transferring functions may be both a blessing and a bane. Neither provides a substitute for metro governance, although both enable at least some local governments in metro areas to cope more effectively with the problems that they individually face.

Annexation is Walker's third middling alternative. Annexation is used by cities to expand their territory and to capture growth that has occurred or is occurring in unincorporated areas outside of the city's boundaries. If a city uses annexation wisely, it can effectively become a regional government because it encompasses all or nearly all of the growth occurring around it. This is the essence of what David

---

5   With the assent of Maryland General Assembly and various governors.

Rusk (1993) has called the elastic city—one that is able to annex practically at will and does so. The reality, however, is that very few cities in the nation make such extensive use of annexation as to establish themselves as regional governments.

Annexation was very common in the nineteenth and early twentieth centuries and remains an option for many cities today, particularly in the south and west. For the most part, it is not available to cities in the northeast and midwest. Moreover, even in states that have fairly liberal annexation laws (for example, cities annex neighboring territory without the affirmative vote of residents of the territory), cities that are surrounded by incorporated areas (that is, other municipal governments) or are bounded by counties of which they are not a part may not be able annex. Where annexation laws are more restrictive and require an affirmative vote of the residents of territories to be annexed, the probability that a city will be able to annex is considerably reduced.[6]

Finally, state constitutional provisions may even prevent certain cities from annexing at all. This is what happened to Baltimore, MD in 1918, when a constitutional amendment was adopted by a statewide vote that effectively eliminated that city's ability to annex (Arnold, 1978). Baltimore, thus, has been confined to its 1918 boundaries, even though considerable growth has occurred in the territories immediately surrounding it. If Baltimore had retained the annexation authority that state law grants to other Maryland municipalities, there is little doubt that the city would have considerably expanded its borders to encompass much of that growth during the last nearly 100 years.

Regional special districts and authorities are Walker's fourth middling alternative. The principal difference between a regional and a local special district is scope. Local districts generally involve one of a few local governments over a territory smaller than an entire metro area. Regional districts, by contrast, can encompass all or substantial parts of a region. However, with a few exceptions, the difference ends here because the districts are generally limited to the provision of a single service and rarely address the tough metro issues. Exceptions include air and water pollution control districts in some states. As is the case of local special districts, regional special districts are both a blessing and a bane and for the same reasons.

In fifth place on Walker's list comes metropolitan, multi-purpose special districts. He distinguished metropolitan special districts from their regional cousins by noting that the former perform numerous functions and services versus the latter performing one or a very few. Walker went on, however, to identify only one such district in the nation at the time of his article—Seattle, WA—and which then performed only two functions, wastewater and public transit. The Municipality of Metropolitan Seattle, however, ceased to exist in 1994 after having been ruled unconstitutional by a Federal District Court for violating the one person, one vote principal of representation. (Its governing board consisted of appointed

---

6 State law is almost certainly the single most important factor influencing the number of annexations that occur in a state. States with more liberal annexation laws see more annexations and vice versa.

representatives from King County and local municipalities in the county.) Metro's functions were taken over by King County (Oldham, 2006). I know of no example today of a metropolitan special district, at least by Walker's definition. Therefore, while in theory this may be an option for local governments to use to address the tough regional issues, in practice it is not.

The reformed urban county is sixth among the middling group of Metro Reform alternatives. Traditional county governments date to the earliest years of American self-government in the seventeenth and eighteenth centuries and were copied extensively from their English predecessors. Traditional county governments operate under state constitutional provisions that mandate the performance of certain functions and services and severely limit these counties' ability to perform other functions and services without either constitutional change or state legislative permission.

Typical names for traditional county governments include board of county supervisors and board of county commissioners, although other names are employed in a few states. A notable feature of this form of county government is that the boards of supervisors or commissioners act as both the legislative and executive authorities of the county. There is no separation of powers. Depending on state law, traditional county governments may also have the authority to appoint professional administrators (similar to city managers in municipal governments).

A reformed county is one that has changed its structure to mirror the structure of a municipality and has also the power to perform what are essentially municipal functions. Reformed counties have locally written charters (like a municipal charter) that describe both the structure of the government and the functions and services that these county governments are permitted to perform. The *charter* county typically has either an elected executive or an appointed manager or administrator and a separate county council or legislative branch. Because its charter describes the functions and services that a county is legally able to provide, the charter county can much more closely mirror the services and functions provided by typical municipalities—hence the moniker *urban county*. Last, unlike the traditional county form of government, except in unusual circumstances, the reformed county does not have to ask for state constitutional change or action from its state legislature to perform urban functions and services or to change those functions and services. The latter is accomplished through amendments to the charter that are voted on by the residents of the county (under state law, of course).

Walker concluded by discussing what he called the *tough trio* or the three Metro Reform alternatives that are most difficult for local governments to adopt. First, he listed the one-tier or city–county consolidations. According to data maintained by the National Association of Counties, since the end of the Second World War (which, of course, marks the beginning of the greatest period of suburbanization in America), there have been 150 attempts at city–county consolidation, of which 32 have been successful—21 percent or about one in five (National Association of Counties, 2014). The great majority of attempted consolidations have occurred

108   *Metropolitan Governance in America*

in the 11 former Confederate states (83 or 70 percent), as have most of the 32 successful consolidations (21 or 67 percent).

Beyond these documented cases, local elites, advocacy groups, local governments and other organizations in countless regions across the country have given at least some consideration to consolidation, but have failed to develop enough support to move it to the next step—development of a consolidation proposal to present to voters.

Most of the attempted and the successful consolidations occurred among relatively small cities and counties in relatively small metro areas or outside of metro areas altogether. See Table 6.2 at the end of the chapter. For example, of the 32 post-war successes, only four occurred in areas with combined populations (city and county) of greater than 200,000 (of which only two in areas with combined populations greater than 500,000). Contrast this with 20 that occurred in areas with combined populations of less than 50,000 (of which ten occurred in areas with fewer than 10,000 inhabitants).

Among other things, this tells us that city–county consolidation does not occur very often—32 times in 68 years among more than 3,000 counties and nearly 19,500 municipal governments. And, it rarely occurs in medium-sized and large metro areas, occurring instead mainly in areas with small numbers of residents. This is probably because the more populous the region, the more complex is its governing structure and more numerous are the stakeholders that would contest over consolidation. The largest city–county consolidation was between Louisville and Jefferson County, KY, in 2000, which in 2013 had a combined city–county population of 609,893 in a metropolitan area of 1,262,261.

As Walker noted, the majority of consolidations have been partial, with at least some suburban municipalities left intact and at least some school districts and special districts untouched. This was also true in the Louisville–Jefferson County consolidation where a staggering number of 83 municipalities remain in operation after consolidation. This suggests that the politics of successful consolidations require that potential opposition be eliminated through various compromises, including carving out territories that will not be absorbed by the consolidation in order to eliminate their opposition to and ultimately their votes against the merger.

The final two of Walker's 17 dwarfs are two-tier and the three-tier restructurings. A two-tier restructuring is akin to the federated approach found in the writings of the Metro Reformers. Here, services and functions are somehow divided between the regional and local levels, with governments at the higher and lower levels providing their respective menu of services and functions.[7] Walker offered Metro Toronto, Ontario, Canada as one example of a two-tier government. The

---

7   To my knowledge, no one has yet figured out how to allocate functions and services without creating enemies—that is, without angering local governments that would lose functions and services to the higher level of government. This is true even though the ACIR devoted considerable attention to doing precisely this (ACIR, 1973).

Ontario provincial government created a regional government for Toronto and its suburbs in 1954 in a top-down act. Since then, the province has reorganized metro Toronto least three times more (1967, 1988 and 1998), with territories being shuffled, boundaries redrawn and services and functions reallocated each time. Additionally, since Walker's article, several additional Canadian cities have been similarly reorganized by their provincial governments, including Ottawa, Hamilton, Halifax, Winnipeg, Montreal and Quebec.

Walker identified Miami–Dade County, FL, as the sole example of a two-tier government in the US. This *metropolitan experiment*, as Sofen called it (1966), began in 1957 with the adoption of a home rule charter by the citizens of Dade County. Today, the metro government (called Miami–Dade) provides a number of services county-wide, provides certain services to the residents of the county's incorporated areas and also provides urban services to the residents in the unincorporated area in the county. The county has 35 incorporated municipalities (with a combined population of 1.28 million out of a total county population of 2.38 million).

The municipal governments provide what are considered "local" functions and services, such as police and fire protection, zoning, code enforcement, and other typical urban services within their jurisdictions. These services are funded with city taxes. Miami–Dade provides a number of services of areawide or metropolitan services (for example, that benefit the entire county), including emergency management, airport and seaport operations, public housing and health care, transportation, environmental services, water and sewer, and solid waste disposal. It also provides services and functions to the county's unincorporated areas. County tax revenues, which are levied on both incorporated and unincorporated areas, pay for these services.

Because of rampant population growth in southeast Florida since the 1950s, Miami–Dade is now essentially an urban county form of government rather than a true metropolitan government as the metropolitan area now encompasses Miami–Dade, Broward and Palm Beach counties (and an additional roughly three million residents). Clearly, however, because Miami–Dade is a structure of government, it engages sub-regional governance over the functions and services that it provides.

Walker's final, and most difficult option, is the three-tier government—three-tier because such governments involve multi-county regions. He cited the Metropolitan Council serving the Minneapolis/St. Paul, MN, region and the Metro serving the Portland, OR, region as the only examples of three-tier governments in the US. At this writing, some 26 later, they remain the only two examples of three-tier governments in the US. So, if I were to revise Walker's classification here, I would move Miami–Dade to the sixth of his middling alternatives, the urban county.

The Twin Cities Metropolitan Council was established in 1967 by the Minnesota state legislature and it has been modified and expanded three times since (1974, 1976 and 1994) also by legislative action. The Metropolitan Council, aka, the Met Council, serves seven counties in Minneapolis/St. Paul metro area.[8] It performs a number of functions and services including a metro transit (bus and rail) system, wastewater collection and treatment, transportation planning, water supply planning and water quality monitoring, land use planning, regional parks, housing policy planning and the provision of a limited number of affordable housing units. Members of the governing board are appointed by the Governor of Minnesota and confirmed by the state Senate.

Initially, there was great optimism that the Council would be able to use its land use and other powers to rein in sprawl in the region. This appears not to have lived up to expectations. Although ranked 16th in population by the Census Bureau among all metro areas in 2010, the Twin Cities metro area is ranked 42nd in weighted population density (Census Bureau, 2010; see also Bradford, 2012).

Perhaps the most innovative Met Council activity is a tax base sharing program for the region. The program has been operational since 1975. Its principal purpose was to reduce fiscal disparities among jurisdictions in the seven county region (the program is actually known as the Metropolitan Fiscal Disparities program). It works by capturing 40 percent of the annual increase in commercial, industrial and public utility property value. In 2013, the program generated nearly $369 million (League of Minnesota Cities, 2014). Funds are distributed from this pool based on a formula that favors poorer jurisdictions over wealthier ones (based on the jurisdictions' per capita property tax value). As one might imagine, this program is somewhat controversial, certainly to the jurisdictions that pay more into the fund and receive less, and there have been attempts to change or even abolish it in recent years. This said, the Council appears also to have sufficient support in the region that its existence, powers and programs (including tax base sharing) are not seriously threatened.

The Portland Metro Council or Metro was established in 1979 (after a 1978 popular referendum) and grew out of the Greater Portland Metropolitan Service District (MSD) and the regional COG (Columbia Region Association of Governments) that preceded it. Metro serves the three Oregon counties immediately surrounding Portland.[9] Initially, Metro was authorized to perform a fairly limited set of services and functions—solid waste disposal and the Portland Zoo. Since then, additional services and functions have been added, including recycling and composting (part of solid waste disposal), public transit, transportation planning (it is the MPO for this region), regional parks, the Oregon Convention Center, the Portland Expo Center and five centers for the arts in Portland, protection of

---

8   The Census Bureau defined metropolitan area consists of 11 counties in Minnesota and two in Wisconsin. The combined statistical area consists of 21 Minnesota and two Wisconsin counties. The Council's jurisdiction includes only seven Minnesota counties. Thus, this is another example of a regional body that does not fully cover its metro area. It is also another example of sub-regional governance (see also Chapter 5).

9   The Census-defined metro area includes five counties in Oregon and two in Washington. Thus, this is another example of a regional entity that does not fully cover the metro area and another example of sub-regional governance (see also Chapter 5).

the region's fish and wildlife habitat, land use planning and maintenance of the region's urban growth boundary.

The latter is the only regional growth boundary in the US, and has been credited with increasing reinvestment inside the urban growth boundary, containing sprawl and with protecting farm land and open space outside of it. Moreover, there appears to be a strong political consensus in the Portland region to retain the boundary (Abbott, 2002).[10]

Unlike the Twin Cities Met Council, Metro is governed by an elected council president and councilors elected from six single member districts (on a one person, one vote apportionment basis). Thus, Metro is the only example of a directly elected governing structure for a regional (really sub-regional) government in the US.

Certainly, the Twin Cities Met Council and Portland's Metro represent the adoption of the Metro Reformers' ideal structures of metro government, and both entities perform a number of valuable services and functions for their respective regions (really, their sub-regions). However, these two bodies represent less than one percent (0.0052, to be precise) of all metro areas in the US. As such, one would be hard pressed to conclude that the three-tier government is any more than very theoretically available to local governments and their residents in US metro areas. This is especially true considering that no other three-tier structures have even been attempted during the 70 years since the end of the Second World War.

To say this does not diminish the value to their regions that these two sub-regional governmental structures add. But it should ground the discussion about whether three-tier structures are likely to be replicable anywhere else in the US. Moreover, there is reason to believe that if the Twin Cities Metro Council did not exist today, it would likely not be instituted by the Minnesota State Government and almost certainly not by the citizens of the region. The Portland Metro, by contrast, appears to have sufficient popular support that if it did not exist today it would likely be adopted.[11]

Conclusion

At least two conclusions can be drawn from this review of Walker's 17 dwarfs regarding these vehicles' ability to promote meaningful Metro Reform. The first is that all 17 alternatives promote at least some measure of reform. However, if we eliminate those that either offer little or no help to local governments in regions to address the tough areawide issues and those that are really not available any longer (for whatever reasons), the number is more like ten than 17, and ten may be somewhat inflated.

---

10 Portland is the 24th largest (in population) metro area in the US and also the 24th most densely populated metro area (Census Bureau, 2010; see also Bradford, 2012).

11 Obviously, this line of argument is difficult to sustain logically due to the absence of a counterfactual in each case.

Here are the ones that I would eliminate and why:

- COGS—The survey clearly showed that they do not engage in regional governance; that a few engage in sub-regional governance; and that many provide some services and functions (though mostly sub-regional). It is also clear that because COGs are creatures of their constituent governments, they are very unlikely to take on controversial issues.
- Federally encouraged regional bodies—For good or ill, the federal government has no urban policy and is decidedly out of the regional governance business.
- State planning and development districts—While these districts, where they exist, probably engage in worthwhile development activities, they do not appear suited to the business of regional governance or of addressing the areawide problems that so energized the Metro Reformers.
- Contracting with the private sector—This is used almost exclusively for service delivery and it is hard to imagine that private sector entities would open themselves to the abuse that would follow if they were to take on the tough, controversial issues in metro areas.
- City–county consolidation—The raw numbers just do not support a conviction that cities and counties are likely to stampede in the direction of the nuptial (that is, the consolidation) chamber any time soon, if ever. There will probably continue to be a trickle of mostly small places that do this. But, even so, because so many metro areas in the US are larger than a single city and county, this alternative does not provide much by way of help for metro reform.
- Two-tier restructuring—This reform was undertaken in the 1950s in one metro area, Miami–Dade, but it is now reduced to essentially an urban county form of government; and no others have been attempted.
- Three-tier restructuring—With the Twin Cities and Portland representing less than 1 percent of US regions and with no other three-tier reforms having been attempted, it is hard to conclude that this alternative offers much real help to the other 379 metro areas.

Second, the remaining ten alternatives do not offer much hope either for meaningful Metro Reform or for the ability of local governments and their residents in metro areas to address issues like sprawl, fragmentation and the negative externalities associated with them. In the body of this chapter, I have discussed why this is the case for each and will not repeat my observations here. Suffice it to say that each one of the remaining ten fails to provide a mechanism to compel local governments to work together to address areawide issues. Yes, local governments can and do cooperate over certain services and functions, but hardly any of those cooperative ventures, agreements with or without teeth, and other structural or non-structural alternatives produce metropolitan governance or otherwise enable the local governments in metro areas and their residents to address the tough areawide problems that they face. In Chapter 7 that follows, I will address the reasons why this is the case. To provide a teaser, it is all about politics and why politics trumps everything else and prevents metro governance from occurring (Norris, 2001b).

A Look at the Evidence 113

Table 6.2   City–County consolidations in the US—1947–2010

Successes (includes percent "pro" vote where available and population[1])		
1947	Baton Rouge/East Baton Rouge Parish, LA (55.1%)	158,236
1952	Hampton & Phoebus/Elizabeth City County, VA (88.1%)	55,028
1957	Newport News/Warwick County, VA (66.9%)	113,662
1962	Nashville/Davidson County, TN (56.8%)	399,743
1962	South Norfolk/Norfolk County, VA (66.0%)	73,647
1962	VA Beach/Princess Anne County, VA (81.9%)	84,215
1967	Jacksonville/Duval County, FL (64.7%)	528,865
1969	Carson City/Ormsby County, NV (65.1%)	15,468
1969	Juneau & Douglas/Greater Juneau Borough, AK (54.1%)	13,556
1970	Columbus/Muscogee County, GA (80.7%)	167,377
1971	Holland & Whaleyville/Nansemond County, VA	35,166
1971	Sitka/Greater Sitka Borough, AK (77.2%)	est. 4,500
1972	Lexington/Fayette County, KY (69.4%)	204,165 (in 1980)
1972	Suffolk/Nansemond County, VA (75.7%)	47,621 (in 1980)
1975	Anchorage, Glen Alps, & Girdwood/Greater Anchorage Area Borough, AK (62.0%)	174,431 (in 1980)
1976	Anaconda/Deer Lodge County, MT (56.0%)	12,518
1976	Butte/Silver Bow County, MT (62.0%)	32,205
1981	Houma/Terrebonne Parish, LA (53.8%)	94,393
1987	Lynchburg/Moore County, TN (93.5%)	4,721
1990	Athens/Clarke County, GA (59.2%)	100,266 (in 2000)
1992	Lafayette/Lafayette Parish, LA (60.0%)	190,503 (in 2000)
1992	Yakutat/Yakuta Borough, AK (90%)	725
1995	Augusta/Richmond County, GA (66.7%)	195,182
1997	KS City/Wyandotte County, KS	161,993
2000	Louisville/Jefferson County, KY	693,604
2000	Hartsville/Troosdale County, TN	7,259

114 *Metropolitan Governance in America*

Successes (includes percent "pro" vote where available and population[1])

2002	Haines City/Haines Borough, AK (55%)	2,392
2003	Cusseta City/Chattahoochee County, GA (60%)	16,078
2006	Georgetown/Quitman County, GA (68%)	3,591
2007	Tribune/Greeley County, KS (73%)	2,275
2008	Preston/Webster County, GA (77.6%)	2,843
2008	Statenville/Echols County, GA (72%)	4,692

Failures (includes percent "pro" vote where available)

1948	Birmingham/Jefferson County, Alabama
1948	Miami/Dade County, FL (45.4%)
1950	Hampton, Newport News, & Phoebus/ Warwick & Elizabeth City Counties, VA
1953	Miami/Dade County, FL (49.2%)
1954	Albany/Dougherty County, GA (28.8%)
1956	Albany/Dougherty County, GA
1958	Nashville/Davidson County, TN (47.3%)
1959	Albuquerque/Bernalillo County, NM (30.0%)
1959	Knoxville/Knox County, TN (16.7%)
1960	Macon/Bibb County, GA (35.8%)
1960	Several cities/Ravalli County, MT
1961	Durham/Durham County, NC
1962	Chattanooga/Hamilton County, TN
1962	Columbus/Muscogee County, GA (42.1%)
1962	Memphis/Shelby County, TN (36.8%)
1962	St. Louis/St. Louis County, MO (40.1%)
1964	Chattanooga/Hamilton County, TN (19.2%)
1967	Tampa/Hillsborough County, FL (25.9%)
1969	Athens/Clarke County, GA (48%)
1969	Brunswick/Glynn County, GA (29.6%)
1969	Roanoke/Roanoke County, VA (66.4%)[2]

Failures (includes percent "pro" vote where available)

1969	Winchester/Frederick County, VA (31.9%)
1970	Anchorage/Greater Anchorage Area Borough, AK
1970	Charlottesville/Albemarle County, VA (28.1%)
1970	Chattanooga/Hamilton County, TN (48.0%
1970	Pensacola/Escambia County, FL (24.6%)
1970	Tampa/Hillsborough County, FL (42%)
1971	Anchorage/Greater Anchorage Area Borough, AK
1971	Augusta/Richmond County, GA (41.5%)
1971	Bristol/Washington County, VA (17.5%)
1971	Charlotte/Mecklenburg County, NC (30.5%)
1971	Memphis/Shelby County, TN (47.6%)
1971	Tallahassee/Leon County, FL (46.9%)
1972	Athens/Clarke County, GA (48.3%)
1972	Macon/Bibb County, GA (39.6%)
1972	Fort Pierce/St. Lucie County, FL (36.6%)
1972	Tampa/Hillsborough County, FL (42.2%)
1972	St. Louis/St. Louis County, MO
1973	Albuquerque/Bernalillo County, NM (44.1%)
1973	Savannah/Chatham County, GA (58.3%)
1973	Tallahassee/Leon County, FL (46.2%)
1973	Wilmington/New Hanover County, NC (25.6%)
1974	Augusta/Richmond County, GA (51.5%)
1974	Charleston/Charleston County, South Carolina (40.4%)
1974	Durham/Durham County, NC (32.1%)
1974	Evansville/Vanderburgh County, IN (26.1%)
1974	Portland/Multnomah County, OR (27.5%)
1974	Sacramento/Sacramento County, CA (24.9%)
1975	Ashland & Catlettsburg/Boyd County, KY (16.7%)
1975	Missoula/Missoula County, MT (46.0%)

Metropolitan Governance in America

Failures (includes percent "pro" vote where available)

1975	Salt Lake/Salt Lake County, Utah (39.0%)
1975	Gainesville/Alachua County, FL (25.2%)
1976	Augusta/Richmond County, GA (45.5%)
1976	Gainesville/Alachua County, FL (32.2%)
1976	Front Royal/Warren County, VA
1976	Macon/Bibb County, GA (32.2%)
1976	Moab/Grand County, UT (21.0%)
1976	Tallahassee/Leon County, FL (45.0%)
1978	Knoxville/Knox County, TN
1978	Morristown/Hamblen County, TN (30.7%)
1978	Salt Lake/Salt Lake County, UT
1979	Okeechobee/Okeechobee County, FL (32.2%
1981	Kingsport/Sullivan County, TN (11.5%)
1981	Clarksville/Montgomery County, TN (16.3%)
1982	Athens/Clarke County, GA (50.2%)[2]
1982	Louisville/Jefferson County, KY (49.6%)
1982	Asheville/Buncombe County, NC (37.7%)
1983	Dublin & Pulaski/Pulaski County, VA
1983	Louisville/Jefferson County, KY (48.1%)
1983	Missoula/Missoula County, MT (24.9%)
1984	Tifton/Tift County, GA (34.8%)
1984	Staunton/Augusta County, VA (59.4%)[3]
1984	Chattanooga/Hamilton County, TN (34.0%)
1985	Volusia Area/Halifax County, FL (44.8%)
1986	Lakeland/Lanier County, GA (34.5%)
1987	Brunswick/Glynn County, GA (51.6%)[2]
1987	Wilmington/New Hanover County, NC (40.7%)
1987	Jackson/Madison County, TN (49.4%)
1987	Clifton Forge & Covington/Alleghany County, VA

A Look at the Evidence   117

Failures (includes percent "pro" vote where available)

1987	Emporia/Greensville County, VA (57.1%)[4]
1988	Sparta/White County, TN (39.4%)
1988	Kingsport/Sullivan County, TN (31.6%)
1988	Augusta/Richmond County, GA Overturned (56.8%)??
1989	Georgetown/Scott County, KY (41.7%)
1989	Frankfort/Franklin County, KY (35.7%)
1989	Conyers/Rockdale County, GA (57.4%)[3]
1989	Okeechobee/Okeechobee County, FL (20.6%)
1990	Gainesville/Alachua County, FL (33.5%)
1990	Sacramento/Sacramento County, CA (43.7%)
1990	Roanoke/Roanoke County, VA (45.1%)
1990	Owensboro/Davis County, KY (28.4%)
1990	Bowling Green/Warren County, KY (23.8%)
1991	Griffin/Spalding County, GA (31.2%)
1992	Ashland &Catlettsburg/Boyd County, KY (33.9%)
1992	Tallahassee/Leon County, FL (40%)
1994	Des Moines/Polk County, Iowa (34.5%)
1994	Douglasville/Douglas County, GA (25.4%)
1994	Metter/Candler County, GA (30.1%)
1995	Wilmington/New Hanover County, NC (41.7%)
1995	Spokane/Spokane County, WA (41.3%)
1995	Bedford/Bedford County, VA (24%)
1996	Clarksville/Montgomery County, TN
1996	Knoxville/Knox County, TN (46%)
1997	Griffin/Spaulding County, GA
1998	Haines/Haines Borough, AK (49%)
2000	McMinnville/Warren County, TN (28%)
2000	Hawkinsville /Pulaski County, GA
2001	Fairbanks/Fairbanks Borough, AK (22%)

Failures (includes percent "pro" vote where available)	
2001	Ketchikan/Ketchikan Borough, AK (42%)
2001	Gainesville, Hall County, GA (47%)
2001	Tullahoma/Coffee County, IN (29%)
2002	Campbellsville/Taylor County, KY
2003	Albuquerque/Bernallilo County, NM (38%)
2004	Des Moines/Polk County, IA (35%)
2004	Albuquerque/Bernallilo County, NM (41%)
2004	Frankfort/Franklin County, KY (25%)
2005	Topeka/Shawnee County, KS (39.5%)
2010	Memphis/Shelby County, TN

1 Population figures are for the nearest census except where otherwise indicated.
2 State law requires majorities in both city and county and referendum failed in the county.
3 State law requires majorities in both city and county and referendum failed in the city.
4 State law requires majorities in both city and county and referendum failed in one of the jurisdictions.

Source: National Association of Counties. 2014. *City County Consolidation Proposals.* Washington, DC: Author. Accessed June 9, 2014, at: http://www.naco.org/Counties/learn/Documents/City%20County%20Consolidations.01.01.2011.pdf.

References

Abbott, Carl. 2002. Planning a sustainable city: The promise and performance of Portland's urban growth boundary. In: Gregory Squires. *Urban Sprawl: Causes, Consequences and Policy Responses.* Washington, DC: Urban Institute Press.

Arnold, Joseph. 1978. Suburban growth and municipal annexation in Baltimore, 1745–1989. *Maryland Historical Society Magazine,* 73(2): 109–128.

Bradford, Chris. 2012 (September 28). The 50 densest American metropolitan areas, by weighted density. Located at the Austin Contrarian blog.http://www.austincontrarian.com/austincontrarian/2012/09/the-50-densest-american-metropolitan-areas-by-weighted-density.html. Accessed October 2, 2014.

Cypher, Trish, and Colin Grinnell. 2007 (August). *Governments Working Together: A Citizen's Guide to Joint Powers Agreements.* Sacramento, CA: California State Legislature, Senate Local Government Committee. www.calafco.org/docs/Senate_LG_JPA_Report.pdf. Accessed October 31, 2014.

League of Minnesota Cities. 2014. *Fiscal disparities 101.* http://www.lmc.org/media/document/1/fd101.pdf?inline=true. Accessed November 29, 2014.

National Association of Counties. 2014. *City County Consolidation Proposals.* Washington, DC: Author. http://www.naco.org/SearchCenter/pages/results. aspx?k=city%20county%20consolidation%20proposals. Accessed October 2, 2014.

Norris, Donald F. 2001a. Whither metropolitan governance. *Urban Affairs Review*, 36(4): 532–550.

Norris, Donald F. 2001b. Prospects for regional governance under the New Regionalism: Economic imperatives versus political impediments. *Journal of Urban Affairs.* 23(5): 557–571. Special issue entitled, "Regionalism Reconsidered."

Oldham, Kit. 2001 (June 18). Metro: Municipality of metropolitan Seattle—HistoryLink.org Essay 7813. Found at HistoryLink: The Free Online Encyclopedia of Washington State History. http://www.historylink.org/index. cfm?DisplayPage=output.cfm&file_id=7813. Accessed October 28, 2014.

Owens, David W. 2014 (May). *Extraterritorial Jurisdiction for Planning and Development Regulation.* Chapel Hill, NC: School of Government, University of North Carolina at Chapel Hill. http://www.sog.unc.edu/node/944. Accessed October 31, 2014.

Rusk, David. 1993. *Cities without Suburbs.* Washington, DC: Woodrow Wilson Center Press.

Sofen, Edward. 1966. *The Miami Metropolitan Experiment*, 2nd ed. Garden City, NY: Anchor Books.

US Advisory Commission on Intergovernmental Relations. 1973–1974. *Substate Regionalism and the Federal System. Volume IV: Governmental Functions and Processes: Local and Areawide.* October, 1973. Washington, DC: US Government Printing Office.

US Bureau of the Census. 2010. Distance profiles for US metropolitan statistical areas, 2000 and 2010. http://www.census.gov/population/metro/data/pop_pro. html. Accessed October 2, 2014.

US Census Bureau, 2012. Census of Governments: Special purpose local governments by state. http://factfinder2.census.gov/faces/tableservices/jsf/ pages/productview.xhtml?src=bkmk. Accessed October 28, 2014.

Walker, David. 1987. Snow White and the 17 dwarfs: From metro cooperation to governance. *National Civic Review*, 76(1): 14–28.

Chapter 7
Conclusion

In drawing this book to a close, I start with a brief reprise of the findings of Chapters 2 through 6. I follow this with a quick review of two recent and somewhat promising ways to conceptualize metro governance—institutional collective action (ICA) and incremental regionalism. Then, I discuss what almost certainly are the principal *political* reasons why metro governance has not been and is not likely to be achieved anywhere in the US. I conclude with my view, based I believe on the available evidence (versus the wishful thinking that characterizes so much of the literature on metro governance) of the likely state of metro governance in the US in decades to come.

Findings from Earlier Chapters

The principal contributions of the Metro Reform School, which I examined in Chapter 2, consist of, first, the identification of a range of problems afflicting metropolitan America. These problems have resulted mainly from the uncontrolled growth in metro areas and their governmental fragmentation, notably in the suburbs. Second, the Metro Reform writers proposed a number of solutions to those problems. Third, there was a high degree of consistency among the Metro Reform writers in terms of both problems and solutions. Finally, however, regardless of their consistency, and often the stridency of their rhetoric, very few metro areas have seen any substantial adoption of metro reforms that might effectively address the tough, controversial problems that they face.[1] This is largely because local governments (and their residents) in America's metro areas are unwilling to sacrifice local autonomy (and tax dollars) on the altar of metropolitan reform and metropolitan governance.

Public Choice theory, which was introduced at about the same time as the Metro Reformers were flourishing and which remains a strong, if flawed, view of metropolitan areas, is singularly unhelpful when discussing metro governance.

---

1 As I have previously noted, these are tough, controversial problems listed repeatedly by the Metro Reformers and the New Regionalists that they also said require areawide solutions: uncontrolled suburban growth; sprawl; governmental fragmentation; loss of open space; traffic congestion; air and water pollution; water supply and distribution; sanitation and solid waste; public education; lack of affordable housing; disparities in wealth, tax base, services and need; segregation by race and class; disinvestment in central cities and their decline; and occasionally others.

Indeed, if one accepts the premises of the Public Choice School, then one rejects metro governance altogether. This is because pubic choice argues that the fragmented metro area is preferable to any alternative to it. As I showed in Chapter 3, the assumptions that underlie the Public Choice model fail to accurately reflect the empirical reality of metropolitan America. Therefore, the model is wrong, any conclusions that may be drawn from it are also wrong, and the model should be rejected. However, the Public Choice model persists, even in the face of years of criticism and scholarship that clearly demonstrates its flaws, largely because of its singular appeal to its adherents within the discipline of economics.

The New Regionalists, whose works began appearing in the late 1980s and early 1990s, argue that local governments in metro areas are impelled to cooperate with one another to ensure that their regions stay competitive in the global economy. As I discussed in Chapter 4, unfortunately for these writers, little evidence exists to support their claims. It is certainly true that American regions inhabit the broader global economy. However, while it is clear that firms compete in the global economy, it is not clear that regions do. Moreover, it is clear by their behavior that local governments do not accept the argument that global economic competitiveness impels them to cooperate. These governments have been no more likely to cooperate since the New Regionalists appeared on the scene—especially around the tough, divisive issues that their regions face—than they were previously. Finally, the New Regionalists' contention that cooperation is a substitute for governance is unsustainable. As so many scholars have shown, cooperation is the weakest of all of the alternatives available to achieve metro governance. As a result, the New Regionalists have been no more successful in achieving any degree of metropolitan governance than the Metro Reformers before them.

I reported the results of my survey of the Councils of Government in the 102 largest metro areas in the US (populations greater than 500,000) in Chapter 5. This survey found no evidence that metropolitan governance occurs anywhere in the US—at least by my rigorous definition of that term. The survey data also showed that metropolitan cooperation, not surprisingly, is widespread and includes both systems maintenance and at least some lifestyle issues. This is also no surprise since local governments in the US have a very long history of cooperation around a wide variety of issues. What is new from these data is the finding of a somewhat larger amount of cooperation around lifestyle issues than expected and reported in previous literature.

Last, the survey found that sub-regional governance occurs in many regions over a variety of issues and across a variety of sub-regional geographies. Sub-regional governance can involve as few as two governments or may involve more. It may address a single or multiple functions. It may include governments in a single or multiple counties. The survey data do not permit an explanation of how, why or to what extent sub-regional cooperation occurs, and this should be on the agenda for future research into metropolitan cooperation and governance.

In Chapter 6, I used David Walker's (1987) list of the major metro reform alternatives available to examine the extent to which local governments deploy them in metropolitan America. Here, I found, unsurprisingly, that local governments have been using many of these alternatives for years and they continue to do so today. However, for the most part the alternatives that local governments have adopted are among the easy ones on Walker's list. As such, these alternatives have little potential to address the tough, controversial issues that metro areas face or to produce metropolitan governance. This is because they mainly involve some form of voluntary cooperation or the creation of single-purpose special district governments.

A few of the alternatives that Walker, and the Metro Reformers before him, proposed have the potential to address the tough issues and to produce metro governance. However, they are exceedingly difficult to adopt, and, therefore, have been adopted in only a few of America's 381 metro areas and generally only on the margins in those areas. This shows, once again, that the metro reforms that are relatively easy to adopt do not do much to address the serious problems facing metro areas and that those that have potential to do so are very difficult to adopt.

Institutional Collective Action

Within the past two decades, an increasing number of works has appeared that describe the theory of ICA. Some of these works also use ICA to guide empirical research into the interactions of local governments in metropolitan areas. According to one of the leading proponents of ICA:

> This theory posits that local governments can act collectively to create a civil society that integrates a region across multiple jurisdictions through a web of voluntary agreements and associations and collective choices by citizens (Feiock, 2010: p.6).

ICA, thus, represents an alternative to the structural reform advocated by previous generations of scholars to address the ills of metro areas. In Feiock's words, ICA promotes a "… path to regional governance based on both cooperation and competition among decentralized governmental units in urban metropolitan areas" (4). Indeed, he also argues that this approach can lead to "decentralized governance" (4).

ICA assumes that local governments, like individuals, have defined interests and can pursue those interests rationally. However, in the decentralized metro area where interests among local governments often diverge, achieving cooperation or collective action can be difficult. If, however, benefits to participants outweigh the transaction costs involved, then collective action is more likely to be achievable (Kwon and Feiock, 2010).

The evidence from the empirical ICA literature clearly shows that local governments in metro areas do cooperate in a number of ways, both formally and informally, over a variety of issues. This finding, of course, is not new. The urban literature has shown for a very long time that local governments cooperate. What is novel about the ICA literature is, first, that it suggests that if the costs of the transactions involved in cooperation can be lowered sufficiently, then more cooperation will occur among local governments in regions. Second, the ICA literature argues that such cooperation can produce regional governance.

The ICA literature also seeks to identify factors that either impede or facilitate cooperation and suggests ways that transaction costs can be reduced to improve the likelihood that cooperation can be achieved (among others, see: Feiock, 2007, 2009, 2010; Hawkins, 2009; Kwon and Feiock, 2010; Olberding, 2002; Post 2010.) However, few, if any, empirical ICA studies go beyond identifying cooperative ventures and the factors that appear to have made them possible. These studies do not examine the cooperative ventures for their performance or effectiveness. Hence, while we know that intergovernmental cooperation occurs over various issues, we do not know whether such cooperation produced the desired results or whether it led to regional governance.

I certainly do not quarrel with the proponents of ICA that it is a useful tool to use to understand and even promote interlocal cooperation in metro areas. Nor would I dispute the value of cooperation to its participants, even though cooperation may not always be an optimal or even an appropriate response to regional problems (Nelles, 2012). However, since ICA is based on voluntary cooperation, it suffers from the same limitations that prior scholarship has shown bedevils this form of interaction. Further, since the mechanisms of cooperation that ICA examines tend to be heavily focused on service provision and often are driven by local governments' desires to achieve efficiency (Feiock, 2007; Kwon and Feiock, 2010), it seems unlikely that regional governance, decentralized or otherwise, will be an outcome.

There may be governance over a particular service among participants in a particular cooperative venture. Indeed, this is likely to be the case, for example, with interlocal agreements (a form of cooperation often examined in the ICA literature). However, any governance here would be limited to the terms of the interlocal agreement, the service involved, the territory included and the time-frame to which the agreement is limited. Therefore, I would consider interlocal agreements (and similar cooperative ventures) as sub-regional governance. As the results of the survey reported in Chapter 5 showed, sub-regional governance is not uncommon. But it is not regional governance. Moreover, as Swanstrom (2001) has noted, cooperation is unlikely to produce governance in American regions because competition is favored over cooperation by the rules of the game as presently constituted.

Finally, it appears to me that ICA is a worthy attempt to circumvent the politics inherent in metropolitan governance. ICA seems to be saying: "If only the transaction costs can be reduced enough, then local governments in metro areas will cooperate over nearly all problems." However, transaction costs may not be the real issue. According to Post (2010), in order for collective action to occur, actors must find it in their self-interests. A considerable problem then with actually achieving regional governance through voluntary cooperation is that most local governments do not find cooperation in their self-interests around the tough, controversial issues that their regions face. This is especially true when cooperation might involve redistribution among or sacrifice on the part of participants. In these cases, cooperation will be difficult or impossible to achieve (Downs, 1994). Finally, as I will show later in this chapter, political factors do not allow transaction costs (if they really are the main barrier to cooperation) to be lowered enough to permit cooperation to occur around the really tough issues.

Incremental Regionalism

Terry Jones and Don Phares have written extensively about regionalism (or its absence) in the St. Louis, MO, metropolitan area. After cataloguing a number of failures to achieve structural reform in this region in a work in 2009, they noted that, despite those failures, the St. Louis region had experienced something that they called *incremental regionalism*. Jones and Phares identified six attempts at major structural reform in the St. Louis region between 1954 and 2006, all involving the City of St. Louis and St. Louis County (legally separate governmental units since 1876). Only one of the six succeeded—formation of a metro sewer district covering the city and the urban portions of the county in 1954, later expanded to cover most of the county. However, during this same period, there were numerous cases of intergovernmental cooperation, including formal agreements, averaging one every two years, around such diverse services and issues as: sanitation, solid waste, education, arts and cultural institutions, public safety, transportation, tourism and sports venues, parks and open space, health care for the indigent and economic development.

Jones and Phares cite six factors to explain why, despite the failures of high-profile reform attempts, these ventures were possible. Few of the ventures were redistributive. Regional learning occurred and made future cooperation easier. *Third rail* issues were avoided. Because of a history of city–county cooperation, transaction costs around successive efforts were reduced. For various reasons (including enlightened self-interest and a desire to be a player), the county with its greater population and affluence joined with the smaller, poorer city to address a number of issues (contrary to the expectation that suburbs will not lend a hand to assist declining center cities). And, finally, crises, such as losing an NFL team, major job losses and declining tourism, forced the city and county to work together around those issues.

However noteworthy this level of intergovernmental cooperation may be, it has mainly occurred between the City of St. Louis and St. Louis County, although a few have involved other jurisdictions in both Missouri and Illinois. None of these ventures, however, is truly metro-wide. Moreover, for the most part, cooperation between the city and county also has occurred around rather easy issues, not the

126 *Metropolitan Governance in America*

tough controversial ones that only true regional governance is likely to be able to address.

Thus, as promising as they may be, neither ICA nor incremental regionalism appears to provide solutions to the dilemmas of regional reform. In the following section, I discuss the reasons why metro reform is so incredibly difficult and why, as a result, metropolitan governance does not exist anywhere in the US.

Political Factors That Prevent Metropolitan Governance[2]

Regardless of the definition or the structures or mechanisms involved, for metropolitan governance to occur, it must be possible for the participants in it to make and implement decisions on issues of regional significance. Decision-making in a polity, any polity, is inherently political in nature. It involves the allocation of scarce resources (Easton, 1965) as well as determining who gets what, when and how (Lasswell, 1950). This being the case, any metro reform will produce winners and losers and, almost the instant that a reform is proposed, will establish two camps around the reform, proponents and opponents. Consequently, it is important to understand those political factors that help to determine which interests populate each camp and how the factors impact the likelihood of success of proposed reforms. In the following paragraphs, I discuss a baker's dozen of the factors that constrain and indeed make major reform to and the areawide governance of America's metropolitan areas nearly impossible to achieve.

American local government ideology

Americans strongly believe that local government, the government closest to the people, is the best government. This rhetoric is, in part, an artifact of American history and, in part, an expression of every day experience. At least since Thomas Jefferson, a central theoretical view of American government has been that of the sovereignty and autonomy of the individual in his or her local community (for example, Syed, 1966).

At a practical level, Americans live in local communities and experience government and governance there. They receive most of their public services, particularly the ones that affect them most significantly (for example, police and fire protection, public education, land use regulation, and so on) at the local level.

---

2 The section on political factors that follows is a based on an article that I wrote for a special issue of the *Journal of Urban Affairs* in 2001 (23(5): 557–571), entitled "Prospects for regional governance under the New Regionalism: Economic imperatives versus political impediments." In 2009, Don Phares and Tanya Zimmerman and I co-authored a chapter, "Metropolitan government in the US and why it is not happening," in Don Phares (ed.), *Governing Metropolitan Regions in the 21ˢᵗ Century?* Armonk, NY: M.E. Sharpe, where, in part, we also expanded on that article.

Citizens are also the most able to make their views about governance and public services known with the greatest impact at the local level. Indeed, the historic and prevailing local government ideology is an important part of the reason why local citizens oppose nearly anything that would threaten the existence, powers, services or autonomy of their local governments.

The residential bias of the American people

Nearly every public opinion poll on the subject shows that large majorities of Americans prefer to live either in suburbs, small towns and or rural areas (see, for example, "Where we'd live," 1989). Additionally, and dating back at least to Jefferson, there is a strong anti-city bias abroad in the land. Americans generally profess to dislike cities, especially big cities. In combination, these attitudes mean that, *ceteris paribus*, Americans not only will move out of and away from cities to suburban and fringe areas, but they will not be kindly disposed to participating in efforts (especially those involving their tax dollars) to help declining central cities. This is true regardless of the merits of such efforts or the dire needs of central cities.

Moreover, since the end of the Second World War, Americans have consistently demonstrated their preferences for residential locations by their behavior. They have chosen the suburbs, where more than half of all Americans currently live (Hobbs and Stoops, 2000).[3] When Americans arrive in the suburbs, and the longer they live there, they show virtually no interest in either assisting the central cities that they have left or surrendering the autonomy and independence of the local governments into which they have moved, regardless of the reason.

Constitutional status of American local governments

State constitutions in the United States expressly provide for the creation of local governments and for the roles and functions of local elected officials. This grant of constitutional and legal status to local governments is fundamentally important. Not only do state constitutions provide the legal basis for local government, by contrast those documents rarely provide a comparable basis for the existence of structures of regional government. In fact, throughout the US, it is far more difficult to establish a regional form of government than to incorporate a new municipality or create a special district. As I have argued elsewhere, both inertia and particular interests grow up around extant local government structures, and they function to favor the status quo over governmental change and reform (Norris, 1997).

---

3 According to the 2010 Census, 85 percent of Americans live in metro areas and, with more than half of Americans living in suburbs, this means that 60 per cent or more of metropolitan residents live in suburbs, so nearly two-thirds of metro area residents live in suburbs. These data show clearly how heavily skewed the population numbers are in favor of the suburbs in any calculation regarding metro reform.

Constitutional and legal status, thus, mean that local governments exist in law; are accorded structure, functions, and powers; and, once established, they beget an existence that is largely unchallenged. Moreover, the existence of local governments helps to preclude the establishment of other governmental structures over the local governments' territories, especially other governments that might threaten the purses or autonomy of local governments. Special districts are allowed; metro government is not.

Territorial imperative

The constitutional and legal status of general-purpose local governments gives them unique territory over which to exercise sovereignty and provide services, and they are loath to share that territory. Yet, in nearly all regions, the territories encompassed by regional organizations, such as regional planning councils and councils of government, include already existing local governments—and the latter are decidedly uninterested in ceding either territory or powers to the former, nor can they be compelled to do so. As such, regional bodies are at a serious disadvantage when compared to local governments that inhabit the regional territory. The former have no independent hold on the territory, while the latter clearly do.

Co-existing within political geography that is fundamentally held by other governmental entities, which also have strong constitutional and legal status as well as strong citizen support, weakens regional institutions for other reasons as well. As I indicated earlier, most of the public services that residents deem important are delivered to them directly by their local governments. Among other things, this means that local citizens have little or no direct contact with regional organizations and are unlikely to think of them as their own governments—if they are aware of the existence of the regional entities or think about them at all. Moreover, most of the officials of local governments that share territory with regional bodies do not feel much ownership in or love for regional bodies. The entities are often seen as remote organizations that do little but are organizations in which they are forced to participate.

The governing boards of the regional bodies are comprised of representatives, usually elected officials, of the constituent local governments. Thus, citizens are not directly represented on governing boards of regional bodies.[4] This makes the regional bodies creatures of the local governments and further removes them from the attention and interest, let alone the direct control, of local citizens. This, in turn, makes it difficult for citizens to attach psychologically or emotionally to regional institutions as they do to their local governments.

---

4   Portland, OR, is the sole exception. Citizens there are directly elected to the regional body.

Conclusion 129

Incorporation and annexation

In much of the nation, state laws and constitutional provisions make it relatively easy for residents of unincorporated areas to create new municipalities through a process known as incorporation. Moreover, once established, it is rare to see even the smallest of these governments abandoned or disincorporated by their residents. As the Metro Reformers noted, this, in turn, has led to the governmental fragmentation of metropolis after metropolis. In any region where incorporated municipal governments surround the central city, that city is essentially land-locked and cannot expand its boundaries outward to capture population and growth in the suburbs. It will have lost its elasticity (Rusk, 1993).

Annexation, as we know from Chapter 2, is the ability of a city to capture growth and development in unincorporated territory outside of its borders. State constitutional provisions and laws vary considerably on the issue of annexation. Either because of these provisions and laws or because of being surrounded by incorporated municipalities, most central cities in northeastern and midwestern metro areas are essentially precluded from annexation, while central cities in the southern and western states have greater latitude to annex.

Cities that annex aggressively have far greater potential to become quasi-regional governments, at least those in smaller metro areas that encompass only a single county. Even in larger metro areas encompassing multiple counties, annexation still enables central cities to capture and even control growth occurring outside of their boundaries. Through annexation, for example, Albuquerque, NM, has captured about 84 percent of the population of Bernalillo County. Albuquerque also represents nearly 63 percent of the population of its four county metro area.

State political tradition. As Berman (1995) noted, although state governments have the constitutional authority to do so, they generally do not get involved in the business of their local governments. Although there have been notable instances of state interference with, and takeovers or near takeovers of local governments or their functions, these are relatively rare.[5] The reasons for states' laissez-faire approach to the operation of their local governments vary, but, for the most part, states establish or provide the mechanisms for the establishment of local governments and expect the local governments to function properly and effectively.

And, in fact, most local governments work reasonably well most of the time. State officials also do not meddle in local affairs without ample reason because they know that to do so would create an unenviable backlash by local voters. Then, too, state officials have their own responsibilities and their state governments to run. As such, and because of both lack of time and inclination, state officials do not want to get into the business of direct service delivery to local residents, and choose to let local governments run themselves.

---

5   Even the most recent state "take over" of an American city, Detroit MI, occurred only after Detroit's financial crisis reached epic proportions, and then lasted only one year and nine months.

Electoral structure and state-elected officials

Another important reason why state governments do not often intervene in local governmental affairs has to do with state and local electoral structure in the US. Many state-elected officials have come up through the lower elective ranks, beginning in local government. They have a healthy respect for local government, and they know that their constituents do as well. Consequently, state legislators are not inclined in the first place to interfere with local governments without good cause.

Additionally, state legislators are elected from local districts that encompass all or parts of one or more local governments. This means that local governments and their residents bring problems and issues and express their policy preferences to their state legislators. This reinforces the legislators' knowledge of and respect for local government and local affairs.

Finally, state legislators are fully aware that if they act, especially without good cause, to intervene in the affairs of local governments (particularly to do anything that adversely affects the territory, finances or powers of local governments), the legislators will almost certainly be opposed at the next primary or general election by local elected officials or local citizens who take serious exception to their actions.

Lack of state and federal leadership or intervention

Unlike Canadian Provincial governments, state governments in the US are reluctant to become involved in reorganizing or reforming their local governments for reasons discussed above. Also for those reasons, it is unlikely that states will suddenly reverse course on a pattern that is many decades old and that, in any event, would be strongly opposed by the residents of the precise local governments that the states would seek to reform.

This, however, does not mean that states will remain passive in the face of serious problems among local governments as the case of Detroit shows. Nor will governors and state legislatures forebear from occasionally passing unfunded mandates and imposing policy burdens on their local governments. However, such actions are mostly motivated by crises, ideology, partisan divisions, or a genuine desire to promote what the instigators believe to be sound and needed policy, rather than to reform local governments.[6] States rarely touch local government boundaries.

---

6   Michigan's imposition of a financial manager on Detroit is a case of a crisis causing state action. In a case of ideology producing state intervention, the Florida legislature adopted a law in 2011 to prevent local governments from making it illegal for persons with conceal carry permits to bring guns into government buildings and to public parks and beaches. This probably also reflects a partisan division in Florida, where the legislature is solidly Republican and many cities, especially in south Florida, are Democratic. In 2012, Maryland state government imposed a storm water remediation fee on the City of Baltimore and the counties bordering on the Chesapeake Bay is what many feel is a case of sound environmental policy but which others decried as a "rain tax."

The federal constitution does not mention local governments nor does it grant the national government any power, authority or role regarding these governments. In the absence of such power, the federal government historically has played no direct role with respect to local government structure and functions.[7] For a very short period of time, from the mid-1960s through the mid-to-late 1970s, led by the US Department of Housing and Urban Development and the US Advisory Commission on Intergovernmental relations, the federal government did attempt to educate, cajole and use its funding ability to encourage local governments in metro areas to work together to address metro-wide problems and issues. And, since the late 1990s, federal transportation funding legislation has required that local governments in metro areas at least pay lip service to regional transportation planning. Beyond these, some might say, feeble efforts, the federal government has played little or no role in the search for solutions to metropolitan problems. Moreover, since at least the 1980s, the federal government has had essentially no urban policy, regardless of the political party that controls the White House.

The strength of pro-sprawl and pro-fragmentation forces

On the rare occasions when the issue of metro reform arrives on the civic agenda in a region, a game (in the sense of the term as employed by Norton Long, 1958), breaks out among the *usual suspects*. This is a game that pits powerful and persistent interests like developers, builders, real estate organizations, suburban residents, and suburban elected officials against less numerous, weaker and transitory interests like academics and *goo-goos* (for example, the good government groups like Leagues of Women Voters, chambers of commerce and editorial writers). The former can be considered the pro-sprawl, anti-reform camp and the latter the pro-regionalism camp. In any contest between these two camps or clusters of interests, the greatest political clout clearly resides with the former who have strong and direct financial interests at stake, who are organized and well-financed, and who have the greatest persistence. The latter, by contrast, are mostly amateurs and volunteers who may have strong intellectual and emotional reasons for involvement, but who are usually poorly organized, poorly financed and who lack the organizational structure and other resources to persist over time. As George Washington Plunkitt said about the municipal reformers of his day, they "were mornin' glories—looked lovely in the mornin' and withered up in a

---

7 However, the federal government can impact local governments in other ways. Like the states, the federal government can and does impose unfunded mandates that affect local governments. One example is the refitting of buildings and other local government infrastructure to meet the requirements of the Americans with Disabilities Act (1990). In addition, through the use of the purse, especially federal grants and the conditions that such grants carry, the federal government can strongly influence local governments (for example, federal legislation in the area of primary and secondary education known as No Child Left Behind, adopted in 2001).

132   *Metropolitan Governance in America*

short time, while the regular machines went on flourishin' forever, like fine oaks" (Riordon and McDonald, 1994: p. 57).

Cross-jurisdictional coalitions that support metro reform may be another category of player in this game (Orfield, 1997, 1998; Weir, 2000). However, with the possible exceptions of Minneapolis and Portland, such coalitions exist hardly anywhere in the US or are too politically impotent to matter in the calculations of the regional reform game.

Race and class

In America, patterns of residential location can be explained partly by likes choosing to live with likes. Were this all that they did, of course, it would hardly be objectionable. However, likes do more than simply choose to live with likes. They also express their preferences through public policies such as land use plans, zoning ordinances and building codes that are often employed or designed to keep the unwanted out.

The unwanted are generally persons of lower socio-economic status and often are non-white. For this and other reasons, suburban areas are increasingly differentiated from their central cities along social class and racial lines. Certainly some suburbs may be poorer or more affluent than others. Likewise some suburbs may be middle class, some working class, and some clearly upper class (as defined by occupation and income); and some may be majority black while others may be majority white. However, suburbs in general are more affluent and more middle and upper class than central cities, with the exception of some older, near-in suburbs. Suburbs are also generally much more likely to have far lower numbers and concentrations of minorities and poor persons than central cities, except, of course, for the growing number of majority–minority suburbs. There is also evidence that, in recent decades, racial and class distinctions as well as income inequality between central cities and suburban areas in the US have become even more extreme (Ellen, 1999; Altschuuler et al., 1999; Lowery, 2000).

Additionally, suburbia as a whole (including recently arrived members of minority groups and lesser affluent residents) does not want to have much or anything to do with the central city, especially if this would mean providing financial support or helping in other ways that could be perceived as threats to the suburbs (such as *fair share* housing). While the suburban, anti-city view is partly due to reasons of race and class, it is also peculiar to suburbanization itself. That is, having escaped the central city, suburban residents (regardless of class or race) do not want to look back and do not want to contribute their time, energy, and especially their tax dollars, to help the central city.

Local government financing and tax structure

On average, the property tax is responsible for about 74 percent of local US governments' tax revenue and 29.7 percent of all local revenue (US Bureau of the Census, 2012). Property taxes produce more own-source revenue for local governments than any other source. Because of the importance of property taxes, American local governments are highly competitive over securing desirable land development, especially commercial and industrial development and upscale housing, within their boundaries.

It is simply not in the interests of local jurisdictions to give away a tax base advantage. Thus, the idea of entering into regional arrangements that might threaten the ability to maximize the generation of local taxes is anathema to local governments. Similarly, local governments are not inclined to support proposals for such things as regional tax base sharing because nearly everyone sees this as a zero sum game. Suburban governments and residents particularly see calls for tax base sharing as ill-disguised bail outs for the central city.

Additionally, varying economic circumstances do not seem to matter to this equation. In good economic times, it is difficult if not impossible to convince local governments to surrender competitive advantage for the good of the whole territory. None of these governments sees the need to do so because all are doing relatively well, and none sees any benefit accruing from his or her individual sacrifice. On the other hand, when economic times are bad across a region or when one or a few local governments in a region are in financial trouble, it is hard to convince those who are well-off to contribute either to the weaker few or to the overall good. Again, the well-off see no benefit accruing from their contribution or surrender of advantage.

Fear of new or higher taxes

Since President George H. W. Bush's famous "Read my lips, no new taxes" statement to the 1988 Republican National Convention, no new taxes has been a political mantra heard frequently and widely across the US. Even before Bush's oft-quoted phrase, however, one of the most damning arguments made by opponents to metro reform was that reform would increase taxes. Residents, especially in suburban areas, feared that city–county consolidations and other proposed metro reforms would burden them with increased taxes to pay for more and higher levels of services and also to bail out the central city. And, as the evidence in Chapter 6 shows, most city–county consolidation proposals in the past 70 years were defeated, and there are no true metro governments anywhere in the nation. At least one of the reasons for this is the fact that the great majority of suburban voters oppose reform, partly over the issue of taxes.

Local government autonomy

Local government autonomy—or the ability of these governments to exercise their police powers (or the power to regulate behavior to protect and enhance public health, safety and welfare) broadly within their territories—is sacrosanct in the US. And, there is absolutely nothing new about this conclusion. It has been

134 *Metropolitan Governance in America*

well known for over 100 years (Danielson, 1976; Teaford, 1979). Indeed, local autonomy is the principal reason that American local governments are unwilling to enter into arrangements for regional governance.

Arrangements for regional governance that would have *teeth*—that is, would involve local governments ceding authority to regional entities to address certain issues, functions and services now under their exclusive control (for example, land use, public safety and public education—would directly threaten local autonomy. As Williams (1967) pointed out, although local governments may be willing to cooperate with one another on matters of systems maintenance (essentially house-keeping and infrastructure matters), they less willing to do so over lifestyle issues, especially if cooperation means any infringement on local autonomy. Nothing much has changed in this regard since the Williams' article appeared nearly 50 years ago.

An example of the power of local autonomy occurred in Maryland in 1997 when then Governor Parris Glendening announced his program of *Smart Growth* for the state. When presenting his initial smart growth plan to local governments in Maryland, Glendening vowed not to interfere with counties' zoning powers (a choice widely viewed as necessary to get the legislation passed). Without significantly curbing local governments' almost exclusive ability to control land development through local land use planning and zoning, anti-sprawl legislation cannot be expected to have much impact. And, indeed, that has been the case in Maryland. Smart growth has not touched local governments' zoning authority, has only barely influenced their land use planning authority, and has done little to curb sprawl in the state.

Another example comes from England where, ten years after the abolition of true metropolitan governments, local governments remained adamantly opposed to regional governance in any form. The most that they would accept, unless forced by central government, were rather minimal levels of cooperation with other local governments in purely voluntary associations which lacked the power to address significant regional issues authoritatively. The principal reason was to preserve local autonomy (Norris, 2001b).

Likely Future of Metro Governance

Calls for metro reform and for greater levels of regional governance are rarely heard in the US any longer, except from the occasional academic or editorial writer. One reason for this is the history of failed efforts to reform metropolitan America. Whether structural reforms proposed by the Metro Reformers or non-structural reforms proposed by the New Regionalists, few reforms have succeeded, and nowhere is there a true metro government in the US.

A second reason is that calls for metro reform are essentially normative arguments. As normative arguments, they assert their advocates' preferences. Although Wood (1958) called the problems of metropolitan areas both "real"

Conclusion 135

and "genuine," he also said: "they are not categorical necessities. They are fundamentally questions of value and of judgment, of what we should and should not do and of how much" (119). He called his approach a normative framework.

The Metro Reformers proposed their reforms simply because they, like Wood, believed strongly that the problems of metro areas were real and genuine and should be addressed. The New Regionalists, who followed, sought to shift the rationale for regional governance away from Metro Reformers' moral imperative to that of regional (and hence local governmental) economic competitiveness. This attempted shift has been insufficient to overcome the powerful political factors that militate against the adoption of both formal structures and informal mechanisms of regional governance. Indeed, because both the Metro Reformers and the New Regionalists failed to take into account the politics of regional governance, their arguments represent little more than wishful thinking.

Even if it were true, for example, that there is, in fact, some moral reason (that is, the greater good of the region) to act favorably on proposals for metro reform or that suburbs and central cities are interdependent or that the economic health of the suburbs is dependent upon the economic health of central cities, participants in the governance of a region would have to accept and act upon these premises in order for the reform proposals to be successful. The participants would have to follow the reformers' logic and adopt and implement the latters' proposed reforms. The available evidence, however, strongly suggests that few, if any, of the participants in metro politics believe in or act on the premises underlying calls for metro reform, regardless of the reform camp from which they emanate.

Additionally, while one may be sympathetic to the goals and objectives of advocates of metropolitan reform and governance, the stark reality is, first, that structural reform has not occurred to any significant extent in metropolitan America, and, second, a regionalism based on voluntary cooperation would be wholly insufficient to produce metropolitan governance. Moreover, this is not happening in any event. As both Lowery (2000) and Swanstrom (2001) have noted, current institutional arrangements in metro areas operate against metropolitan governance. Swanstrom put it this way: "It is unlikely ... that cooperative governance arrangements will arise spontaneously in American regions as presently constituted. The present rules of the game ... favor competition over cooperation" (492).

This is because these and other policies advocated by those who would reform metro areas—redistributive in nature, as they are—generate opposition from both urban and suburban participants in the region's governance who perceive them as threats. Hence, they refuse to participate in such policies and, because their participation is voluntary, they can make their refusal stick.

Consequently, regional governance under voluntary cooperation is nearly always a victim of the lowest common denominator phenomenon. Any single unit can scuttle decisions made and policies adopted for the good of the overall territory (see, Norris, 2001a). Only strong regional governance (one that could produce and compel compliance with decisions) would be sufficient to produce policies that would achieve the goals of metro reform. Thus, contrary to the claims of the New Regionalists and more recently by scholars advocating institutional collective action and incremental regionalism, it is most unlikely that metropolitan governance can exist without metropolitan government.

Writing more than 40 years ago, Wood (1958) endeavored to forecast what regional governance, circa 1975, might look like. After reviewing what he believed to be the salient trends affecting metropolitan America in 1958, Wood wrote:

> There are not enough reliable data over a long enough period of time to weigh the relative pulls of metropolitan dominance [metropolitan reform] and grassroots renaissance [metropolitan fragmentation]. But, there are enough data to allow us to be sceptical [sic] of the one community hypothesis [whether a single metropolitan "community" might come into existence] (118–119).

Today, ample data are available to suggest quite strongly the primacy of separation, competition and fragmentation over metropolitan reform, of whatever stripe. In a particularly telling example, in 1998 Wyly, Glickman and Lahr examined the ten top trends affecting American cities and metropolitan areas. A trend toward metro reform or regional solutions to urban problems or regional governance was not among them. If one were to catalogue the principal urban and metropolitan trends today, it is highly unlikely that such a trend would be observed either.

The third and primary reason for the absence of metropolitan governance in the US is to be found in the political impediments previously discussed. Because of these impediments, there simply is considerable opposition to and insufficient support for metropolitan governance nearly everywhere in the country. If this conclusion is correct, and the evidence presented in this book strongly suggests that it is, the next question is where should the debate over metropolitan governance proceed from here? What, if anything, can be done to strengthen metropolitan governance given the certainty that, in framing this issue, politics trumps both a normative and an economic rationale for it.

Four choices appear to be available. The first is a continuation of the current rhetoric for metropolitan reform. That this rhetoric has not been successful in producing much, if any, meaningful metro governance anywhere in the US since at least the 1930s, however, might suggest that such an approach will not succeed.

Second, there is a laissez-faire option that would essentially accept the Public Choice position that the fragmented metropolis is, indeed, an efficient mechanism for allocating public values, and take no further action. This may, in the final analysis, be the smart choice. It certainly seems to be the most practical and least frustrating, especially given the nature, strength and persistence of the political impediments to achieving metro governance.

However, it would be a wholly unsatisfying choice for many urbanists because it would admit that efforts to address real and genuine metropolitan problems must be abandoned. A laissez-faire approach would also mean, irrespective of the objective data about inter- and intra-metropolitan inequities, central city and inner tier suburban decline, and a host of other well-known metropolitan problems, no ameliorative or remedial action should be advocated or taken.

A third approach is to seek ways to strengthen voluntary cooperation. In 1987, Walker suggested several alternatives to regional governance *with teeth*. His list contained at least 13 options that did not involve governmental reform in metropolitan areas. He also noted that many, if not all, of those options were in use in metropolitan areas throughout the US. As shown earlier, however, there are two principal drawbacks to voluntary cooperation. First, cooperation lacks the power to compel compliance, and, second, it suffers from the lowest common denominator phenomenon.

Might it be possible, though a combination of incentives and disincentives, to strengthen cooperation? In other words, to give it teeth? In theory, of course, this might be possible. But the available evidence suggests that, as a practical matter, it is unlikely to happen. I use as data points the following: 1) the relative lack of success of metropolitan planning commissions and councils of government, and the like, even when they had A-95 review authority, to do much to affect control of land use in metropolitan areas or to affect solutions to other areawide problems; 2) the relative failure of MPOs under federal transportation legislation to do much more than cobble together regional transportation plans based on the desires of individual jurisdictions (versus committing to regional transportation planning based on addressing the needs of the overall territory); and 3) the withdrawal of the federal government from supporting regional approaches and solutions. Thus, cooperation will remain the weakest and least effective means of achieving anything resembling regional governance.

A fourth possible option presents itself in the role of state government. Gainsborough (2001) identified several means by which state governments could facilitate regionalism, and Frisken (2001) has shown that the success of regional governance in the Toronto area was largely the result of actions by the Ontario Provincial government. Both Gainsborough and Frisken, however, also noted an important limitation to the role of state or provincial government—political will. As Gainsborough (2001) said, "any rule is only as strong as the political will to maintain it" (510). Thus far, state governments in the US have shown little interest in or willingness to pursue metropolitan reform. Moreover, as Gainsborough notes, even when states act to facilitate regionalism, regional cooperation is easier to achieve on systems maintenance than lifestyle issues.

Where does this leave the matter? My conclusion is decidedly pessimistic. Because of the formidable political factors that hinder its development, the probability of achieving metropolitan governance anywhere in the U. S. in the foreseeable future is no better than it has been over the past 85 years or more. At least the probability is very low in the absence of a sustained crisis or crises that might somehow require the local governments in a region to cede some of their local autonomy and cooperate in meaningful ways or which might require senior levels of government to step in and force some form of metropolitan governance. Clearly, however, history is not very sanguine that such will occur.

Advocates of metropolitan governance of all types will undoubtedly continue their calls for metropolitan reform and metropolitan governance, and undoubtedly they will achieve a victory from time to time. Based on current trends, however, a reasonable forecast for the state of metropolitan governance in the US 20 or 50 years from now or more would be that it will closely resemble its current state. The political impediments to metropolitan governance will remain strong, and American metro areas will continue to be sprawling, governmentally fragmented entities resistant to nearly all efforts to reform them and to achieve metropolitan governance.[8]

References

Altschuler, Alan, William Morrill, Harold Wolman and Faith Mitchell. 1999. (Eds) *Governance and Opportunity in Metropolitan America.* Washington, DC: National Academy Press.

Berman, David. 1995. Takeovers of local governments: An overview and evaluation. *Publius*, 25(3): 55–70.

Danielson, Michael. 1976. *The Politics of Exclusion.* New York: Columbia University Press.

Downs, Anthony. 1994. *New Visions for Metropolitan America.* Washington, DC: Brookings Institution.

Easton, David. 1965. *A Systems Analysis of Political Life.* New York: Wiley.

Ellen, Ingrid G. 1999. Spatial stratification within US metropolitan areas. In Alan Altschuler (Ed.), *Governance and Opportunity in Metropolitan America.* Washington, DC: National Academy Press.

Feiock, Richard C. 2007. Rational choice and regional governance. *Journal of Urban Affairs*, 29(1): 47–63.

Feiock, Richard C. 2009. Metropolitan governance and institutional collective action. *Urban Affairs Review*, 44(3): 356–377.

Feiock, Richard C. 2010. Introduction: Regionalism and institutional collective action. In Richard C. Feiock (Ed.), *Metropolitan Governance: Conflict, Competition, and Cooperation.* Washington, DC: Georgetown University Press.

Frisken, Frances 2001. The Toronto story: Sober reflections on fifty years of experiments with regional governance. *Journal of Urban Affairs*, 23(5): 513–541.

Gainsborough, Juliet F. (2001). Bridging the city-suburb divide: States and the politics of regional cooperation. *Journal of Urban Affairs*, 23(5): 497–512.

Gray, Virginia and Peter Eisinger. 1997. *American States and Cities* (2nd ed.). New York: Longman.

---

8 This is essentially a repetition of a prediction that I made in an earlier work about metropolitan governance (Norris 2001a). Little, if anything, has changed since then for me to consider revising that prediction.

Jones, Terry and Don Phares. 2009. Moving toward regional governance incrementally. In Don Phares (Ed.), *Governing Metropolitan Regions in the 21st Century*. Armonk, NY: M.E. Sharpe.

Hawkins, Christopher V. 2010. Competition and cooperation: Local government joint ventures for economic development. *Journal of Urban Affairs*, 32(2): 253–275.

Kwon, Sung-Wook and Richard C. Feiock, 2010. Overcoming barriers to cooperation; Intergovernmental service agreements. *Public Administration Review*, 70(6): 876–884.

Lasswell, Harold D. 1950. *Politics: Who Gets What, When, How*. New York: P. Smith.

Long, Norton E. 1958. The local community as an ecology of games. *American Journal of Sociology*, 64(3): 251–261.

Lowery, David. 2000. A transactions costs model of metropolitan governance: Allocation versus redistribution in urban America. *Journal of Public Administration Research and Theory*, 10(1): 49–78.

Nelles, Jen. 2012. *Comparative Metropolitan Policy: Governing beyond Local Boundaries in the Imagined Metropolis*. London: Routledge.

Norris, Donald F. 1997. Local government reform in the US—And why it differs so greatly from Britain. *Local Government Studies*, 23(3): 113–130.

Norris, Donald F. 2001a. Prospects for regional governance under the new regionalism: Economic imperatives versus political impediments. *Journal of Urban Affairs*, 23(5): 557–571. Special issue entitled, "Regionalism Reconsidered."

Norris, Donald F. 2001b. Whither metropolitan governance? *Urban Affairs Review*, 36(4): 532–550.

Norris, Donald F., Don Phares and Tonya Zimmerman. 2009. Metropolitan government in the US and why it is not happening. In Don Phares (Ed.), *Governing Metropolitan Regions in the 21st Century*. Armonk, NY: M.E. Sharpe.

Olberding, Julia C. 2002. Does regionalism beget regionalism? The relationship between norms for regional partnerships for economic development. *Public Administration Review*, 62(4): 480–491.

Orfield, Myron. 1997. *Metropolitics: A Regional Agenda for Community and Stability*. Washington, DC: The Brookings Institution and the Lincoln Land Institute.

Orfield, Myron. 1998. Conflict or consensus: Forty years of Minnesota metropolitan politics. *Brookings Review*, 16(4): 31–35.

Post, Stephanie S. 2010. Metropolitan area governance and institutional collective action. In Richard C. Feiock (Ed.), *Metropolitan Governance: Conflict, Competition, and Cooperation*. Washington, DC: Georgetown University Press.

Riordon, William L. and Terrence J. McDonald. 1994. (Ed.). *Plunkitt of Tammany Hall: A Series of Very Plain Talks on Very Practical Politics*. Boston, MA: Bedford Books of St. Martin's Press.

Rusk, David. 1993. *Cities without Suburbs*. Washington, DC: The Woodrow Wilson Center Press.

Stoops, Frank and Stoops, Nicole. 2000. Demographic Trends in the 20th Century. Washington, DC: US, Census Bureau. www.census.gov/prod/2002pubs/censr-4.pdf. Accessed December 27, 2014.

Swanstrom, Todd. 2001. What we argue about when we argue about regionalism. *Journal of Urban Affairs*, 23(5): 479–496.

Syed, Anwar H. 1966. *The Political Theory of American Local Government*. New York: Random, House.

Teaford, John. 1979. *City and Suburb—The Political Fragmentation of Metropolitan America, 1850–1970*. Baltimore, MD: Johns Hopkins Press.

Walker, David B. 1987. Snow White and the 17 dwarfs: From metro cooperation to governance. *National Civic Review*, 76(1): 14–29.

Weir, Margaret. 2000. Coalition building for regionalism. In Bruce Katz (Ed.), *Reflections on Regionalism*. Washington, DC: Brookings Institution Press.

Where We'd Live. 1989 (October 21). *National Journal*, p. 2602.

Williams, Oliver P. 1967. Lifestyle values and political decentralization in metropolitan areas. *Southwest Social Science Quarterly*, 48(4): 299–310.

Wood, R. C. 1958. Metropolitan government, 1975: An extrapolation of trends—The new metropolis: Green belts, grass roots or gargantua? *American Political Science Review*, 52(1): 108–122.

Wyly, Elvin K., Norman J. Glickman and Michael L. Lahr. 1998. A top ten things to know about American cities. *Citiscape*, 3(3): 7–32.

US Bureau of the Census. 2012. *Census of Governments. State and Local Government Finance Summary Report*. http://www.census.gov/govs/local. Accessed December 27, 2014.

US Census Bureau. 2014. American Fact Finder: Annual Estimates of Resident Population. http://factfinder.census.gov/faces/tableservices/jsf/pages/product view.xhtml?src=bkmk. Accessed December 27, 2014.

Index

Italic page numbers indicate tables.

1400 Governments: The Political Economy of the New York Metropolitan Region (Wood) 17–18

A

adoption of meaningful reforms 122–3
    annexation 105–6
    city-county consolidations 107–8, 112, *113–18*
    classification of alternatives 99–100, *100*
    Councils of Government (COGs) 102–3, 112
    extraterritorial powers 102
    federally encouraged single-purpose regional bodies 103–4, 112
    interlocal service agreements 100–1
    joint powers agreements 101–2
    metropolitan special districts 106–7
    one-tier consolidations 107–8, *113–18*
    private sector, contracting with 104, 112
    reformed urban counties 107
    regional special districts and authorities 106
    state planning and development districts 104
    three-tier consolidations 109–11, 112
    transfer of functions 105
    two-tier consolidations 108–9, 112
    voluntary cooperation 100–1
Adrian, C.R. 32
Advisory Commission on Intergovernmental Relations (ACIR) 18–19, 21, 24–6, 27–8, 29–31
African-Americans, mobility of 38
All in It Together (Ledebur and Barnes) 68

Alternative Approaches to Governmental Reorganization in Metropolitan Areas (ACIR) 21
alternative approaches to regional governance 122–3
    annexation 105–6
    city-county consolidations 107–8, 112, *113–18*
    classification of alternatives 99–100, *100*
    Councils of Government (COGs) 102–3, 112
    evaluation of 112
    extraterritorial powers 102
    federally encouraged single-purpose regional bodies 103–4, 112
    interlocal service agreements 100–1
    joint powers agreements 101–2
    metropolitan special districts 106–7
    one-tier consolidations 107–8, *113–18*
    private sector, contracting with 104, 112
    reformed urban counties 107
    regional special districts and authorities 106
    state planning and development districts 104
    three-tier consolidations 109–11, 112
    transfer of functions 105
    two-tier consolidations 108–9, 112
American local government ideology 126–7
annexation 105–6, 129
autonomy of local governments 133–4
    and cooperation 64
    and New Regionalism 72–3

B

Banfield, E.C. 32
Barnes, W.R. 67–8
Bembry, J.X. 39
Berman, D. 129
Birmingham, England 72–3
Blair, J.P. 70
bounded rationality theory 39
Bradbury, K.L. 69
Buchanan, J.M. 49

C

Chamber of Commerce of the United
    States 16–17, 26–7
charter counties 107
cities
    anti-city bias 127, 132
    city-county cooperation 84, 85
    county-city consolidations 1947-2010
        113–18
    global city-regions (GCRs) 74–5
    suburban dependency 67–70
city-county consolidations 112
    1947-2010 *113–18*
    adoption of 107–8
class 132
Committee for Economic Development
    (CED) 28
competition
    global economic 62–7
    public choice theory 51
    between regions 63–6
constitutional status of local governments
    127–8
cooperation
    city-county cooperation 84, 85
    decision-making 63–4
    differences between actors 64
    extent of 87, *87, 92,* 92–3
    formal/informal 86, *86,* 91–2
    global economic 60–1
    institutional collective action (ICA)
        123–5
    and negative externalities 66
    New Regionalism 61–2, 73–4
    non-profit sector involvement in 88,
        88, 93, *94*
    Poland 73–4

and politics and autonomy of local
    governments 64
private sector involvement in 88, *88,*
    93, *94*
in self-interest, capabilities in 66
and size of population 90–5, *91, 92,*
    93, 94
strengthening 137
survey findings on *85,* 85–90, *86, 87,*
    88, 89, 90
voluntary, adoption of 100–1
voluntary, as weak 64
Councils of Government (COGs) 102–3,
    112
county-city consolidations
    1947-2010 *113–18*
    adoption of 107–8
county governments 107

D

decision-making, regional 63–4
Di Salvo, P. 40
diseconomies of scale 43
Dowding, K. 40, 52

E

Easton, David 2
economics and global economic
    cooperation 60–1, 62–7
efficiency as principal value in Tiebout
    model 48–9
electoral structure 130
England, New Regionalism in 72–3
Ermisch, J. 40
European research on New Regionalism
    71–5
extent of cooperation 87, *87, 92,* 92–3
extraterritorial powers 102

F

federal leadership, lack of 130–1
federally encouraged single-purpose
    regional bodies 103–4
Feiock, R.C. 123
financing of local governments 132–3
firms, regions equated with 65–6
formal/informal cooperation 91–2
freedom 48

Friesma, P. 32
Frisken, F. 75, 137

G
Gainsborough, J.F. 137
Glasgow, Scotland 71
global city-regions (GCRs) 74–5
global economic cooperation 60–1, 62–7
Goetz, Ch. J. 49
Goodall, L.E. 32–3
governance in America
   fragmentation and overlaps 1
   governance/government distinction
      61–2
Governing the Metropolis (Greer) 19–20
government/governance distinction 61–2
*Government of Metropolitan Areas in the
   United States* (Studenski) 9–11
*Governmental Structure, Organization and
   Planning in Metropolitan Areas
   1961* (ACIR) 18–19
governments in America, number of 1
Greer, Scott A. 10–20
Gulick, Luther 13–14, 23–4

H
Hill, C.A. 38, 54
Hill, E.W. 69, 70
Holland 71–2
house prices, regional differences in 38
Howell-Moroney, M. 48, 49

I
incorporation 129
incrementalism regionalism 125–6
information, perfect 40–1
institutional collective action (ICA)
   123–5
integration 10–11, 20
interlocal service agreements 100–1, 124

J
joint powers agreements 101–2
Jones, Victor 11–13

K
Kantor, R. 71–2, 74–5
Kay, A. 37, 39–40, 52–3, 54

knowledge about tax-service packages
   40–1

L
Lackowska, M. 73–4
Ladd, H.F. 42
Lakewood Plan 46, 101
Ledebur, L.C. 67–8
legal status of local governments 127–8
lifestyle/systems maintenance services and
   functions 87–8, *88*, 93
local governments
   American ideology 126–7
   constitutional status of 127–8
   number of to choose from 41–2
   revenue received by 44–5
   similarity between 42
localism and public choice theory 50
Lowery, D. 39
Lyons, W.E. 39

M
Manchester, England 72–3
market, metropolis as 35–6
Marsh, A. 37, 39–40, 52–3, 54
Martin, Roscoe C. 22–3
*Metropolis in Transition: Local
   Government Adaptation to
   Changing Urban Needs* (Martin)
   22–3
*Metropolitan America: Challenge to
   Federalism* (ACIR) 24–6
metropolitan areas
   capacity of to address problems 10
   defined 1
*Metropolitan Disparities and Economic
   Growth* (Ledebur and Barnes)
   67–8
metropolitan governance
   absence of, reasons for 134–7
   defined 2–3
   future for 136–8
   size of COGs 80
   see also survey of metropolitan
      governance
Metropolitan Government (Jones)
   11–13
'Metropolitan Government' (Wood) 14–15

metropolitan planning organizations (MPOs) 82–4, 102–3
Metropolitan Problem and American Ideas, The (Gulick) 23–4
Metropolitan Reform School 121
   1400 Governments: The Political Economy of the New York Metropolitan Region (Wood) 17–18
   adoption of solutions, likelihood of 11, 13, 15–16, 18, 20, 21, 24, 25–6, 27, 31
   Advisory Commission on Intergovernmental Relations (ACIR) 18–19, 21, 24–6, 27–8, 29–31
   Alternative Approaches to Governmental Reorganization in Metropolitan Areas (ACIR) 21
   capacity of metropolitan areas to address problems 10
   Committee for Economic Development (CED) 28
   compared to New Regionalism 62
   criticism of 32, 46
   Governing the Metropolis (Greer) 19–20
   Government of Metropolitan Areas in the United States (Studenski) 9–11
   Governmental Structure, Organization and Planning in Metropolitan Areas 1961 (ACIR) 18–19
   Gulick, Luther 13–14
   integration 10–11, 20
   Metropolis in Transition: Local Government Adaptation to Changing Urban Needs (Martin) 22–3
   Metropolitan America: Challenge to Federalism (ACIR) 24–6
   Metropolitan Government (Jones) 11–13
   'Metropolitan Government' (Wood) 14–15
   Metropolitan Problem and American Ideas, The (Gulick) 23–4

Modernizing Local Government 1960 (Chamber of Commerce of the United States) 16–17
Modernizing Local Government 1967 (Chamber of Commerce of the United States) 26–7
negative externalities 9–10, 12, 18, 23–4, 28
New Regionalism as expanding work of 59
population growth, problems with 9–10, 12, 14–15, 15, 16, 17, 18, 19–20, 21, 23–4, 24, 26, 27, 28, 29
preferences of residents 32
procedural adaptations 22
Regionalism Revisited: Recent Areawide and Local Responses (ACIR) 30–1
Reshaping Government in Metropolitan Areas (Committee for Economic Development) 28
similarities between works of 7, 31–2
solutions to problems 10–11, 12–13, 14, 15, 16–17, 17–18, 18–19, 20, 21, 22–3, 24–5, 26–7, 27–8, 28, 30–1, 31–2
structural adaptations 22
Substate Regionalism and the Federal System Vol. 1 (ACIR) 29–31
Suburbia: Its People and Its Politics (Wood), Robert C. 15–16
Urban America and the Federal System (ACIR) 27–8
metropolitan special districts 106–7
mobility of citizens
   African-Americans 38
   job-related moves 42
   and public choice theory 37–40
Modernizing Local Government 1967 (Chamber of Commerce of the United States) 26–7
Modernizing Local Government (Chamber of Commerce of the United States) 16–17

N

National Association of Regional Councils (NARC) 79

Index

negative externalities 18
  cooperation, capabilities of 66
  effectiveness against, survey findings
    89, *89,* 94, *94*
  Metropolitan Reform School 9–10, 12,
    18, 23–4, 28
  New Regionalism 60
  Tiebout model 42–4
New Regionalism 122
  autonomy of local governments 72–3
  Birmingham, England 72–3
  compared to Metropolitan Reform
    School 62
  competition between regions 63–6
  cooperation 61–2, 73–4
  cooperation between regions 63–6
  England 72–3
  European research on 71–5
  as expanding work of Metropolitan
    Reform School 59
  firms, regions equated with 65–6
  focus of 59
  Glasgow, Scotland 71
  global city-regions (GCRs) 74–5
  global economic cooperation 60–1,
    62–7, 75
  governance/government distinction
    61–2
  lack of working examples 75
  Manchester, England 72–3
  negative externalities 60
  objectives of 60
  Poland 73–4
  and politics 72–3
  Randstad, Holland 71–2
  suburban dependency 61, 67–70
non-profit sector involvement in
    cooperation 88, *88,* 93, *94*
normative aspects of Tiebout model
    48–51
Norris, D.F. 39, 75
number of governments
to choose from 41–2
more governments as better in public
    choice theory 50–1

O

Oates, W.E. 42

optimal community size in Tiebout model
    44
Orfield, M. 66
Ostrom, Vincent 45–7

P

parochialism in Tiebout model 43
perfect information 40–1
planning, transportation 82–4
Poland, New Regionalism in 73–4
politics
  and absence of metropolitan
    governance 136
  American local government ideology
    126–7
  annexation 129
  anti-city bias 127, 132
  autonomy of local governments 133–4
  class 132
  constitutional status of local
    governments 127–8
  and cooperation 64
  electoral structure 130
  fear of new of higher taxes 133
  financing of local governments 132–3
  incorporation 129
  institutional collective action (ICA)
    124–5
  and New Regionalism 72–3
  pro-sprawl/pro-fragmentation forces
    131–2
  race 132
  residential bias of American people
    127
  state-elected officials 130
  state/federal leadership, lack of
    130–1
  state government, role of 137
  state political tradition 129
  tax structure 132–3
  territorial imperative 128
polycentric government. *see* public choice
    theory
population growth problems, Metropolitan
    Reform School on 9–10, 12,
    14–15, 17, 18, 19–20, 21, 23–4
population size and cooperation levels
    90–5, *91, 92, 93, 94*

146 Metropolitan Governance in America

populations, factors influencing changes
in 45
Post, S.S. 70, 124
preferences of residents
Metropolitan Reform School 32
and mobility 37–40
private sector
contracting with 104, 112
involvement in cooperation 88, *88,* 93
procedural adaptations 22
property taxes 132–3
public choice theory 121–2
assumptions based on 36–45, 53
competition among local governments
as good 51
diseconomies of scale 43
economic thinking as paramount 51
efficiency as principal value 48–9
expansion of Tiebout model 45–7
freedom 48
job-related moves 42
knowledge about tax-service packages
40–1
limitations of 35
literature reviews 52–3
localism as better 50
longevity of, reasons for 54
market, metropolis as 35–6
mobility of citizens 37–40
more governments as better 50–1
negative externalities 42–4
normative aspects of Tiebout model
48–51
number of governments to choose from
41–2
optimal community size 44
public goods and services focus 49–50
purpose of 36
revenue received by local governments
44–5
sorting of citizens 38–9
validity and utility of 53–5
public goods and services, public choice
theory's focus on 49–50

R
race 132
Randstad, Holland 71–2

rational choice theory 39
reform of metropolitan governance
absence of, reasons for 134–7
annexation 105–6
city-county consolidations 107–8, 112,
113–18
Councils of Government (COGs)
102–3, 112
extraterritorial powers 102
federally encouraged single-purpose
regional bodies 103–4, 112
interlocal service agreements 100–1
joint powers agreements 101–2
metropolitan special districts 106–7
one-tier consolidations 107–8, *113–18*
private sector, contracting with 104,
112
reformed urban counties 107
regional special districts and authorities
106
state planning and development
districts 104
three-tier consolidations 109–11, 112
transfer of functions 105
two-tier consolidations 108–9, 112
voluntary cooperation 100–1
see also Metropolitan Reform School
reformed urban counties 107
Regional Councils 102–3
regional special districts and authorities
106
*Regionalism Revisited: Recent Areawide
and Local Responses* (ACIR) 30–1
*Reshaping Government in Metropolitan
Areas* (CED) 28
residential bias of American people 127
revenue received by local governments
44–5
Rossi, P.H. 40
Rusk, David 105–6

S
Savitch, H.V. 60, 63, 68–9
Scotland 71
service agreements 101
size of communities, optimal 44
smaller governments in public choice
theory 50

sorting of citizens and public choice theory 38–9
special districts 30, 104–5
   metropolitan 106–7
   regional special districts and authorities 106
state-elected officials 130
state government, role of 137
state leadership, lack of 130–1
state planning and development districts 104
state political tradition 129
Stein, R.M. 38, 70
Stephens, G.R. 42
structural adaptations 22
Struggling Giants: City-Region Governance in London, New York, Paris and Tokyo (Kantor) 74–5
Studenski, Paul 9–11
sub-regional governance 83
Substate Regionalism and the Federal System Vol. 1 (ACIR) 29–31
suburban dependency 61, 67–70
Suburbia: Its People and Its Politics (Wood), Robert C. 15–16
suburbs, anti-city bias of 127, 132
survey of metropolitan governance
   city-county cooperation 84, 85
   cooperation, findings on *85*, 85–90, *86, 87, 88, 89, 90*
   definition of metropolitan governance 81
   extent of cooperation 87, *87*, 92, 92–3
   formal/informal cooperation 86, *86, 91*, 91–2
   methodology *80*
   metropolitan governance, findings on 81–5
   negative externalities, effectiveness against 89, *89*, 94, *94*
   private/non-profit sector involvement 88, *88*, 93, *94*
   purpose of 79
   regions of respondents 80–1
   representativeness of respondents 79–80, *80*
   response rate *80*
   size of population 90–5, *91, 92, 93, 94*

sub-regional governance 83
summary of findings 122
systems maintenance/lifestyle services and functions 87–8, *88*, 93, *93*
Swanstrom, T. 63, 70
systems maintenance/lifestyle services and functions 87–8, *88*, 93, *93*

T
tax base of local governments 44–5
taxes
   fear of new of higher 133
   property 132–3
territorial imperative 128
three-tier consolidations 109–11, 112
Tiebout model
   assumptions based on 36–45, 53
   competition among local governments as good 51
   diseconomies of scale 43
   economic thinking as paramount 51
   efficiency as principal value 48–9
   expansion of 45–7
   freedom 48
   job-related moves 42
   knowledge about tax-service packages 40–1
   limitations of 35
   literature reviews 52–3
   localism as better 50
   longevity of, reasons for 54
   market, metropolis as 35–6
   mobility of citizens 37–40
   more governments as better 50–1
   negative externalities 42–4
   normative aspects of 48–51
   number of governments to choose from 41–2
   optimal community size 44
   parochialism 43
   public goods and services focus 49–50
   purpose of 36
   revenue received by local governments 44–5
   smaller governments as better 50
   sorting of citizens 38–9
   validity and utility of 53–5
tight labour market hypothesis 69

transfer of functions 105
transportation planning 82–4, 102–3
two-tier consolidations 108–9, 112

U

United States, Poland comparison with
      73–4
Urban America and the Federal System
      (ACIR) 27–8
urban counties 107

V

Vogel, R. 60, 63
Voith, R. 68

voluntary cooperation, adoption of 100–1

W

Walker, David 99–111, *100,* 137
Warren, Robert 45–7
Weir, M. 66
Wikstrom, N. 42
Williams, O.P. 134
Wood, Robert C. 14–16, 17–18, 134–5,
      136
work and mobility of citizens 42

Z

Zhang, Z. 70